REAL FAITH

REAL FAITH

WHAT'S AT THE HEART OF THE GOSPEL?

JOHN MURRAY

AMBASSADOR INTERNATIONAL
GREENVILLE, SOUTH CAROLINA & BELFAST, NORTHERN IRELAND

www.ambassador-international.com

REAL FAITH

What's at the Heart of the Gospel?

© 2012 by John Murray
All rights reserved

Printed in the United States of America

ISBN: 978-1-62020-042-1
eISBN: 978-1-62020-043-8

Unless otherwise indicated, Bible quotations are taken from The New International Version of the Bible. Copyright 1978 by the New York Bible Society.

Cover Design by Justin Hall
Page Layout by Justin Hall

AMBASSADOR INTERNATIONAL
Emerald House

427 Wade Hampton Blvd.
Greenville, SC 29609, USA
www.ambassador-international.com

AMBASSADOR BOOKS
The Mount
2 Woodstock Link
Belfast, BT6 8DD, Northern Ireland, UK
www.ambassador-international.com

The colophon is a trademark of Ambassador

×

DEDICATED TO

My children, Susan and Glenn,

and to my daughter-in-law Beth,

whose lives have been an outstanding spiritual example and an exemplary

blessing to their families.

×

There are two

special people I would like to acknowledge

in the preparation of this book.

✕

Firstly, my wife Rita, who was always an encouragement

in the progress of the book but more than that, she became a wonderful

sounding board as we discussed the comprehension of theological issues—

often over breakfast, much to her chagrin!

Her insights proved invaluable.

✕

The other person is our good friend Barbara Kerkhof,

who, as a professional proof-reader, added my manuscript

to her extracurricular work.

Her conscientious and meticulous work

was an incredible asset and probably saved me

from abject embarrassment.

Praise for
REAL FAITH

"Addressing common questions about the triune God – Father, Son and Holy Spirit, Christian conversion, and the challenges and expectations of Christian living, John Murray provides an introduction to essential Christianity. Writing with clarity and accessibility, Murray guides the all-ready committed to a deeper understanding of their faith and the seeker to a clearer picture of what it means to be a Christian."

David Daniels
Pastor,
Grace Baptist Church,
Richmond Hill, Ontario, Canada.

✕

"John Murray in *Real Faith: What's at the Heart of the Gospel?*, moves us to consider the foundation of faith, speaking to the issues Christians frequently face. His purpose is to answer '…those questions which bring perspective to the Christian faith.' He takes faith as an ethereal idea and brings it into our living. Beginning with 'Why do we believe?' he poses questions with stories and responses that lead naturally into questions for group study. This helps a reader, or a group, wrestle with how one thinks and what one believes. I recommend you take advantage of his work and turn it into a rich and faith-building moment."

Dr. Brian C. Stiller
Global Ambassador
World Evangelical Alliance

✕

"Though the world be inundated with information, it is vital to communicate those words and ideas that will be significant long after this information-flooded age has passed away. And this book succeeds admirably in doing just that as Scripture and stories from the author's own life, are woven together to form a fine introduction to the rich world of Christian thinking and experience."

Dr. Michael A.G. Haykin
Professor of Church History and Biblical Spirituality,
The Southern Baptist Theological Seminary,
Louisville, Kentucky, U.S.A.

"Writing out of his own rich experience of the Christian life, John Murray has provided us with a book that is intended to orient those who are relatively new to the faith to the great truths of Christianity. It is written in a conversational style and tackles some important questions. It promises to be particularly helpful to those who are trying to square difficult circumstances with their faith.

"The book could be described as the author's own creed—but it is more than that. John lives a cheerful and victorious Christian life and has an infectious joy. He has had to face adversity himself and, as a former Executive Director of Eurovangelism, he has ministered to a section of the church experiencing harsh persecution. He has discovered by personal experience that true Christianity works in the bad times as well as the good times. I commend this book for its balance, its warmth, and its honesty. It is not only an interesting read but also a very helpful one."

Dr Ellis Andre
Senior Pastor
White Rock Baptist Church
British Columbia, Canada

✕

"This is a clear, straightforward, biblically solid, believer's guide to the basics of the Christian faith. Rather than a series of analytical theological lectures, the author, instead, walks as a guide with the reader, succinctly describing with deep conviction the major, wondrous riches of Christian doctrine.

By addressing the questions, including tough ones, commonly raised by those newly committed to Jesus Christ, this work provides a fine, readily accessible introduction to the complete orb of the Christian faith and life into which they are entering. For longer term followers of Christ, this overview is not only a helpful review but may also bring to light some aspect of the faith of which they were previously unaware, or neglected, or perhaps even shunned, and will inspire further pursuit of an even deeper understanding of faith in, and commitment to, Jesus Christ."

Dr. T.R. Anderson
Emeritus Professor of Theology and Christian Social Ethics,
Vancouver School of Theology,
Vancouver, Canada

FOREWORD

Faith is a journey. A journey towards a deeper understanding of who we are as spiritual beings, a journey into a deeper knowledge of who God is, a journey in which the important questions of life find reasonable answers. It is the journey of joining our story to God's story, a journey that goes from here to eternity.

It has been said that 'Faith is not a blind leap into the dark, but an open eyed step into the light.' Faith is always a step, but it is a reasonable, rational, and intelligent step! No one can prove the existence of God, but the evidence of his footprints on the path of our journey is clearly seen for those who have eyes to see. His fingerprints are all over this planet and the people on it. This book 'Real Faith' which you have in your hands will help you on your journey to see those footprints and recognize whose fingerprints they are.

Faith is one of those aerosol words that we spray around which mean so many different things depending on the context. There is My Faith, The Faith, People of Faith, Authentic Faith, Believing Faith, Healing Faith, Personal Faith etc., and now here John refers to 'Real Faith'! Well, our faith needs to be real, that's for sure. We need to have a faith which affects our daily living. This is where John has done such an excellent job in asking the key questions for which we need clear answers. He writes with a beautiful balance of head and heart which makes it that much easier to transfer it to our hands and feet.

As I write this, it is early in 2012, which happens to be the year of the summer Olympics in London England, the city of my birth! Paul was very familiar with the Olympics and was probably thinking of them when he wrote his letter to the church in Philippi. He says "Forgetting the past and looking forward to what lies ahead, I press on to reach the end of the race and receive the heavenly prize for which God, through Christ Jesus, is calling us" Philippians 3:12 -15 NLT.

Paul is describing himself as an Olympian in the Olympic final of a long distance race. The race is well under way but it's not yet over, there are a few laps still to go. He may have come a long way and covered much ground, but he is still pressing on to learn more, to do more and to become more like his Jesus. This book 'Real Faith' invites you to do the same. I encourage you to continue on in your journey, to make your faith more real. May the Holy Spirit quicken these pages, and your spirit, to make that a reality in your life?

Dr Justin Dennison
VANCOUVER, CANADA

PREFACE

Here we are, early in the twenty-first century, and Christians around the globe are being despised, ostracized, and persecuted for their faith. Hundreds, if not thousands, have been killed and some even beheaded. Does this not seem reminiscent of 500 years ago? The message of the Christian faith is not welcomed or accepted in many countries. It is in direct opposition to the thinking and philosophy of today's secular society. The gospel is incompatible with present day standards so that sooner or later, Christians intent on living out their faith will experience conflict. It's not always a physical confrontation; more often, it comes in the form of intellectual opposition. The thinking and actions of Christians are increasingly questioned and challenged. This book, *Real Faith*, opposes those who suggest that the Christian faith is not only a crutch for the weak-minded or escapism for the timid but also that it is insignificant in its demands. Those with this mindset know very little about Christianity, its experience, or its history.

One's motivation to write is often birthed in experience, and this book is no different. Although I am no theologian, as a Christian I do desire to know what I believe and why. For too long, many of us have simply accepted what we have been taught, because of who did the teaching. We respected our parents, our teachers, and our elders in general. Not that the teaching was wrong or misconstrued, but we need to understand for ourselves the basis for the Christian truth transmitted to us. I believe it is important that we understand the "whys" of our beliefs and have some reasoning for it all. How can we ever give a reason for what we believe if we are not clear about what we believe?

When I became a Christian, I would have liked to have understood what had actually taken place. Over the years I have discovered that others, like me, were brought to the point of embracing the Christian faith, but then we were left to our own devices to grow. We would not expect a baby to feed itself and find its own way in life. Yet it seemed as if we were expected to learn all about the Christian faith by spiritual osmosis. To ask searching questions was not always well received. This is not uncommon among Christians still today.

How I wish that, as a teenage Christian, I had received a book that outlined the basic tenets of the Christian faith and what was really expected of me. This book is written with that purpose in mind. As young people, we were reluctant to show our ignorance, so questions often remained unasked and unanswered. Maybe your experience has been similar.

I have made an honest attempt to answer those questions that bring perspective to the Christian faith. I hope you will gain a better understanding of what Christianity is all about and what actually takes place when you become a believer in Christ. This is not a new concept or new view, but I have tried to present the Christian faith in simple terms without losing the wonder of its magnificence. As we recognize that magnificence, it should bring excitement as we live out the gospel. As you read, I hope you grasp a new vision of the privileged and powerful position you have in Jesus.

How can we be expected to fulfill our role as Christians if we are unsure of what that role is? How did we arrive in this position, and what took place to get us here? How can we build a house without first laying the foundation? To carry out our awesome responsibility in this world as Christians, we need to understand the reasoning and purpose of that responsibility. Knowing that should deepen our faith and solidify our walk with Christ and allow us, as ordinary people, to enjoy extraordinary living.

1

WHY DO WE BELIEVE?

"Everyone who believes in him may have eternal life."
JOHN 3:15

Paul was single, thirty years of age, and very successful as a New York day trader. He had arrived in New York a few years earlier from his home town of Portland, Oregon. He had a fairly conservative upbringing. His father was a chartered accountant, while his mother had never worked outside the home. His only sibling, a brother, was married and had established a teaching career in a city not far from Portland. Paul's mother would attend church on special occasions such as Christmas and Easter, and she would invite Paul to go along with her, which he did when he was young but later decided against it. His father always put forth the idea that "church was for children and old ladies," although he never explained his reasons for such a view. He occasionally took great delight in quoting the words of Karl Marx, "Religion is the opium of the people," although, again, never discussing the subject any further.

Living in New York was a far cry from life in Portland for Paul. He would leave his luxury condo in Manhattan each morning to take up his position at his day-trading office. He was virtually glued to the screen of his computer. During the trading day, he rarely left his desk except to replenish his coffee. Paul's regular schedule after work took him to the local gym and then on to a local bar for the "happy hour" before having supper at home or at a local restaurant. His evening was occupied with reading or some television. He had some good friends whom he mainly saw either at the "happy hour" or over the weekend, although he gave much of his weekend to catching up with the financial newspapers and magazines in preparation for another week's trading.

One morning Paul was preparing to leave for the office when, suddenly, he was sideswiped mentally by this question: "What am I doing, and why am I doing this?" He had no idea what triggered the thought. He immediately realized that for months on end, each day passed by the same as the day before. He felt as if his life was on a treadmill. He could not figure out why these questions were suddenly coming to mind, although he realized that attending the recent funeral of a friend killed in an accident had left him in a strange, questioning mood. Until that moment, Paul could not remember whether any specific questions like these had ever arisen before.

Life had been good to him. He had everything he wanted. He had money in the bank, a superb sports car, a luxury condo, great friends, and a good occupation that was his passion. But now he found himself faced with the question, "What is the purpose of all this?" He asked himself, "Is this truly what life is all about?" He thought, "Am I really thinking all this because of the funeral?" Another thought came to him. "Maybe it really doesn't have anything to do with religion. Maybe I just need to find for myself some kind of philosophy of life!"

The questions kept coming. It was as though he could not help himself. Wanting to find some satisfactory answers, he wondered with whom he might speak without appearing foolish or stupid. He thought to himself, "I need to find someone who will not think my questions crazy or off the wall." He remembered a fellow trader called Brian who was always talking about his church and his faith. Brian always seemed to be level-headed and have everything together. So Paul decided, for good or bad, he would approach Brian with his questions.

Later that morning as he stood at the coffee machine, Paul began a deliberate search for answers to these perplexing questions on his mind. Paul hesitantly opened the conversation with Brian. "I'm not sure how to start this off, but let me ask you this—do you think that this is all there is to life?"

"What do you mean, Paul?" said Brian.

"Well, look at what we do. We come to work, we earn money. We go away, spend it, buy the stuff we want, and then come back for more of the same. Is this truly what living is all about?" asked Paul.

"That's good, Paul. I like what I am hearing. You are one of the few guys around here who is beginning to look at life more seriously," Brian responded. He went on, "I think you have come to know where I stand. I believe that there is a real purpose to life. I believe that our existence is not just an accident of the cosmos but that God determines our existence. I believe that he made us for himself, to know him and be known by him. I also believe that we will only find complete satisfaction once we have established a personal relationship with God."

"But how do you know that God exists?" Paul responded.

"How do you know the wind exists, Paul?" was Brian's quick reply. "You can't see it, but you believe in it. Why?"

"Well, I guess there is evidence of it even though we cannot see it."

"Precisely."

"But the subject of God is much bigger than the wind, Brian." Paul leaned against the wall.

"That is true, but it does show that many people believe in something they cannot see, like oxygen or air or gravity. They find it hard to explain, but they have no doubt about their existence."

"Well, I still would like to hear how you know there is a God..."

"You know," Brian interrupted, "millions of people have asked the same question before you, Paul. I don't think the answer is as simple as being provided with a formula or attempting to give a couple of convincing items of evidence. Each person becomes convinced of God's existence through different means. I can only talk from personal experience, so let me say that God has proven himself to me many times in my life, and consequently, my faith in him has been confirmed and solidified. It wasn't always that way, however, and it hasn't always been smooth sailing. There have been times of doubt when life has hit me hard, but ultimately, I have always discovered that God was there. It was I who became absent, if you understand what I mean?"

"Yes, I believe I do," Paul replied, pushing away from the wall, "but it all sounds so simple and easy when you talk about it. I really would like to learn more. I have to go now, but could we meet again?"

"Better than that, Paul," said Brian with a smile. "There is someone I would like you to meet. A man who is very well-educated and can answer your questions much better than I can. Would you be willing to have coffee with my pastor? His name is William Birch—Doctor Birch, actually—but everyone calls him Bill. Would you be willing to do that?"

"Well, sure, I guess so," replied Paul with a little hesitancy. "I wasn't quite expecting that; but I guess he, if anyone, should be able to answer some of my questions."

"Good," said Brian. "Then I'll give him a call later and get you together with him."

SEARCHING

Most of us can readily identify with Paul because that's where some of us started our journey to faith. At some point in our lives, we probably faced the same questions and others like them: "Who am I? Why am I here?" These questions often materialize after we experience a wake-up call such as a near accident or, like Paul, a friend's funeral, particularly where someone has died unexpectedly. I read once that not until we face death do we look at life seriously. For others, it might be the proverbial mid-life crisis or a family or relationship crisis, maybe a serious illness or the loss of a parent or spouse. It seems that when we are reminded of our own mortality, questions of life come to mind. These situations lend themselves to our asking such questions and wondering how we fit in.

Surprisingly, we all have some vague answer to these questions, even without being fully aware of it. In our subconscious, we have formed answers to these questions based upon our existing view of life, answers that may leave us feeling uncomfortable.

We all have a philosophy of life; it determines the way we live. We have principles and uphold certain values, particularly as they relate to other people. We all have a worldview; this determines the way we see things around us and the way we interpret life. Rarely are we asked to define that philosophy or worldview, and therefore, it mostly remains in the subconscious and non-verbalized. It is not until we begin to ask the great questions of life that our personal philosophy, or view of life, is forced to come to the surface. As we proceed through life, we acquire and formulate opinions on life and death. Yet there are people who avoid asking these "first order" complex questions of life for fear of finding out the answers.

In the book *Right Thinking in a World Gone Wrong*, John MacArthur shares the story of being on a hike and meeting a young man who was living in a large cardboard box high up in the California mountains. Upon talking with him, John MacArthur discovered that the young man had been educated at Boston University and had seemingly run away from life. When asked if he had found the answers he was looking for, the young man replied, "No, but I have escaped, and I don't have to face the questions!"[1] But the questions do not go away.

SIGNIFICANCE

Deep down, man has an insatiable desire to find meaning and purpose for his existence. He feels inwardly driven by this quest. Some people call it a search for significance. Significance is inevitably tied to the questions of "Who am I?" and "Why am I here?" Significance is important to us. There are very few of us who do not yearn for it. Maybe it's just a desire to be personally recognized by others, or perhaps we want to achieve something significant in our lifetime. None of us wants to be a meaningless speck floating on the ocean of life or a blip on the universal radar screen. We want to know that, ultimately, we have made a difference by being here. We would like to know that the world is a better place because of our presence. We desire to leave our mark after we have gone, to know that we have written our name on the wall to say, "I was here!" These are the factors that motivate and drive us in our search for meaning and significance.

The common understanding of significance in twenty-first century society is to have power, wealth, and possessions, and to be recognized for it. As you probably are aware, this is called "the good life." Our society believes that money in the bank, owning property, owning exotic cars, and enjoying a luxurious lifestyle creates significance in the eyes of others; to some degree this is right, because that belief appears to be universal. The motivational gurus of our day put forth their message that you can "have it all" with the mantra of "If you can think it, you can achieve it!" Billions of dollars are spent by people seeking time and financial freedom. They attend lectures and conventions. They buy courses that supposedly hold the secret to incredible wealth—only to find that the wealth has gone to those offering the secrets.

The billionaires and millionaires of our day are usually held in high esteem because of the size of their bank accounts rather than for their contribution to society. Even those who make substantial contributions to the less fortunate are still revered by the public, not for their philanthropic activity, but because they are rich. This confirms the concept that money and possessions carry significance. Yet some biographies of "rich men" tell another story. They discover that their money is not enough to bring personal satisfaction and significance.

Some commit suicide because their lives are meaningless even in the midst of their wealth.

I remember a friend talking to me about job satisfaction. He had held some leadership positions in the corporate world, but he displayed a sense of frustration about his life. He indicated that in spite of all his success—the position, the cars, the houses he possessed—he would readily change places with me for the fact that my mission work in Eastern Europe held far more purpose and satisfaction than anything he had ever achieved. He was seeking an answer for the meaning and purpose of his life. He was beginning to wonder what kind of mark he would leave behind.

Seeking answers to the questions of life is really a spiritual quest. For centuries secular philosophers have attempted to answer these "big" questions of life but with little success. Their published findings often appear to be the result of groping in the dark. Some readily admit that life appears to be pointless, with little purpose except to be born, procreate, and die. In fact, I read that some philosophers have admittedly given up trying to define the purpose and meaning of life. Others conclude that life is a perpetual circle, or the existence of man has no meaning, that we are nothing more than a "cosmic accident."

That secular philosophers have trouble with these issues is understandable. It is because they seek to obtain answers that pertain to the spiritual world by studying the physical world. This view is myopic and limited. It has been likened to a man trying to find out how a box is made by looking only inside the box. The box was made from the outside. Secular philosophers can only see the inside of the box because that is where they are. Because the answers are spiritual, it calls for a spiritual examination from the outside of the box. The answers do not lie within us, as some would like to suggest.

The humanistic view suggests that the divine is within man and simply needs to be awakened by a concentrated thought process.

Salvation and significance for the humanist begins with man, is achieved by man, and ends with man. The New Age movement offers a similar view. They offer so-called spiritual attainment through meditation, utilizing various natural phenomena in an attempt to induce some state of tranquility. It all sounds so wonderful, which is why, sadly, many are attracted and fooled by its concepts. But the significance and meaning of man's existence can never be found within himself.

Our belief systems hinge on the existence or non-existence of God. If one has no belief in God, then there can be no Christian belief system. However, if we believe in the existence of God, then we have no option but to face the question of how God's existence relates to us and how we relate to him. We have no other choice. Facing the truth of this issue is not easy, though, because accepting the existence of God brings with it an uncomfortable accountability. However, we need a reason for our existence.

To find real meaning and purpose in life, we are forced to look beyond the bounds of our own limited minds. Because the answer is spiritual, it is only in God that we will find the answer which satisfies. Without God, life becomes meaningless. Without God, life does not make sense. Without God in the picture, life is a puzzle. God created man for himself, so that all of life pertains to God. Without this understanding, we can never make sense of life and its purpose. God the Creator is Spirit, and so to understand life, we must understand the things of the Spirit. Unfortunately, in the natural, man cannot understand things spiritual.

SATISFACTION

It was the seventeenth century philosopher Blaise Pascal who suggested that there is a God-shaped vacuum within the heart of man. Therefore, until this vacuum is filled with a proper relationship with God, we miss life's greatest purpose. This is exactly why philosophers who ignore this aspect of the divine have no success in making sense of man's existence. They are trying to fit together a jigsaw puzzle with a giant piece missing. In one of his prayers, St. Augustine expressed these words to God: "Our hearts are restless until they find their rest in thee." Without God, man lives in a state of helplessness and hopelessness and also often in a state of catatonic ignorance. God provides the anchor and is the anchor. Without him, we flounder around in a sea of senseless man-made concepts.

Regrettably, since man was birthed, he has chosen to avoid or ignore God to his own peril. We can choose to reject God, ignore God, or discount his existence, but it does not change the facts. It's like truth. Truth is not dependent upon our views or opinions. It is not dependent upon our interpretation. Truth exists as truth in spite of us. So whether we know the truth or accept the truth, it makes no difference to the truth. Truth exists without our knowledge, belief, or acceptance. So, man's deliberate refusal to accept the truth of God's existence only affects man and not God. It is man who denies himself a relationship with God.

Bertrand Russell, the well-known British atheist, when asked what he might say to God if after death he discovered that he had been wrong in his thinking, replied, "Why, I should say, 'God, you gave us insufficient evidence!'" According to the Scriptures, Russell was wrong in his atheistic thinking and also wrong regarding his insufficient evidence. The existence of God is clear from creation itself, by the order of things in the world and by the mountains of uncontested evidence revealing that God is alive and is active in the world. It is extraordinary to think that man chooses to ignore the evidence and live in a state of suspended understanding of who he is and why he exists.

SOLUTION

God created us for more than just what we see around us, more than just what occupies us day to day. In his book *A Quest for More*,

Paul David Tripp states that God "constructed us to live for more than ourselves. He designed us to want meaning, purpose and consequence. We were not wired to be fully satisfied with self-survival and self-pleasure. God purposed that the borders of our vision would be much, much larger than the boundaries of our lives. We were meant to see more than our physical eyes can see, and it is that greater vision that was meant to engage, excite, connect and satisfy us."[2] Because we have been created for more, we continue our search for more.

We desire something outside of ourselves, that inexplicable "something" which we sense will satisfy that inner craving for significance. We spend time and money in pursuit of the elusive achievement. It appears to be a moving target. Man can only find meaningful answers to his searching questions by going to the very source of his life, God himself. God made man in his image, for himself, and until man looks in the right place, his search will be endless and fruitless. His search will only end through the experience of Christian conversion. That may sound too definitive, but if God made man for himself, then there can be only one answer, which is to "know God" and to establish a personal relationship with him.

God created us to experience a personal relationship with him, and until that relationship is established, there will always be a sense of dissatisfaction or lack of fulfillment. We may have climbed the corporate ladder, been outstanding in our achievements, and even made millions of dollars, but all that is quite superficial and useless if a spiritual hunger persists. Millions of people are searching for the truth but are looking in the wrong places. Consequently, they have not yet experienced the extraordinary living that God has made available.

Although "knowing God" holds different connotations for different people, it carries a similar essence as in knowing anyone—it is the establishing of a personal relationship with him. Once we have established relationships with human friends, we are free to say that we know them. This is what happens when we come to know God through Christian conversion. We shall look at this in more detail later, but suffice it to say now that we were born to know God and be known by him. Simply having an academic understanding or knowledge of God without a spiritual relationship with him is like being fully aware of how to swim but unable to actually do it. Some people cannot understand or even comprehend such a relationship with God. However, such a spiritual relationship can only be understood through the work of God's Holy Spirit. By his work, he takes us from the possibility to the reality. Such a spiritual experience is not created simply through head knowledge; it's much deeper than that.

So, considering the chapter title, why do we believe? It is inherent in all of us to believe. It is in our nature to believe. We believe because we are made for belief. We are made to worship God—hence the number of different religions around the world. Man is on a continuous search for reconciliation with God, whether he knows it or not. This is the reason why we believe. This is the reason we continually search for answers to the questions about life, about ourselves, and about what comes after this life. Let us see what our Christian faith has to say about these things.

×

QUESTIONS FOR GROUP STUDY:
WHY DO WE BELIEVE?
Reading: Matthew 19:16–30

1. Describe what you think is the difference between an atheist and an agnostic.

2. Do you think everyone has a belief system or a world view in place? Give your reasoning.

3. Describe what kind of activities or events in life might cause people to think seriously about the Christian faith and why such events work in that way.

4. Can people be won over to the Christian faith by logic? If so, how? If not, why not?

5. What helped formulate your present belief system? Has it changed over the years?

6. What do you consider should be presented to non-believers as an introduction to the Christian faith? It needs to be something that captures their attention and interest.

2

WHAT ARE THE PILLARS OF CHRISTIANITY?

"Guide me in your truth and teach me."
PSALM 25:5

When I was young, we owned a three-legged stool in our home, the kind used to milk cows—not that we had any cows to milk! I cannot remember how, but I do know that one of the legs got broken. Whether one of my brothers threw it at me or I threw it at them, I'm not sure; I do know this: once it had lost one of the legs, it was of no more use. It could not stand straight and was only good for firewood or throwing away. Nothing could be supported by the stool once one of the legs was broken. Likewise, Christianity stands on three legs. Remove one of them and you not only have an inoperable faith, but you have no evangelical Christian faith at all. I purposely say evangelical Christian faith because there are groups who would consider themselves Christian without holding in totality to these three aspects of Christian doctrine.

These are the three pillars upon which the Christian faith is built: the existence of God, the Trinity, and the divine inspiration of the Bible. Take any one of these away and there would be no real Christian faith. Because this book is written for Christians of evangelical persuasion, it is assumed that these three aspects of doctrine are readily accepted and believed. Therefore, a full and complete explanation is not planned here.

Nevertheless, because of their importance, it would be remiss of me not to give a brief summary of these foundational truths before moving on to consider further details of the Christian faith.

THE EXISTENCE OF GOD

It makes logical sense that anyone who expresses a Christian faith believes in the existence of God. As the Scripture says, "Without faith it is impossible to please God, because anyone who comes to him must believe that he exists and that he rewards those who earnestly seek him" (Hebrews 11:6). Thus, this is the first pillar of Christianity: believing in the God of the Bible. Millions of people believe in the existence of a god—in fact, many gods—but we refer here to the biblical concept of the one, true God.

It has been said that probably the greatest and most important question that anyone can ask is this: "Does God exist?" The answer is crucial because it forms the basis upon which we build our whole belief system. In the previous chapter, the question was raised of how one can believe in God without outward physical evidence. It is true that we cannot see God, but we are not without outward evidence. No one would dispute the existence of the wind after a tornado has passed through a town. Jesus referred to the wind in John 3:8 when he said, "The wind blows wherever it pleases. You hear its sound, but you cannot tell where it comes from or where it is going." Yet we believe in its existence. No one disputes the existence of gravity when they see the result of a rockslide, an avalanche, or a can of paint falling from a scaffold. The evidence is indisputable. Yet we cannot see gravity. Thus with God, we have the Scriptures and life itself that give us conclusive evidence of the existence of God.

For the Christian, God's existence is an indisputable fact supported by the overwhelming evidence given in creation, nature, science, and astronomy. Scores of books have been written confirming the unique and exquisite design of the universe and the delicate balance within the order of creation. We learn that the world has been perfectly placed in the universe to create an environment to sustain life on earth. Even secular astronomers and scientists are admitting to an intelligent design within the universe and are almost embarrassingly faced with the evidence of a Creator.

Hugh Ross, in his book *The Creator of the Cosmos,* quotes Allan Sandage, a winner of the Crafoord Prize in astronomy (equivalent to the Nobel Prize), who remarked, "I find it quite improbable that such order came out of chaos. There has to be some organizing principle. God to me is a mystery but it is the explanation for the miracle of existence, why there is something instead of nothing."[1] God has revealed himself and goes on revealing himself. Many choose to ignore the evidence to their disadvantage.

The book of Romans provides a first-class explanation of man's refusal to accept that evidence. In highlighting this fact, it states, "What may be known about God is plain to them, because God has made it plain to them. For since the creation of the world God's invisible qualities—his eternal power and divine nature—have been clearly seen, being understood from what has been made, so that men are without excuse" (Romans 1:19-20).

In his book, *In Understanding Be Men,* Archdeacon T.C. Hammond states, "There is a world-wide intuition in the heart of man that there is a Supreme Being who is to be worshipped. Although this intuition expresses itself in very many different ways .... Its existence provides strong evidence of the existence of God." He goes on to say that "the existence of God is fundamental to our thinking."[2] The understanding of humanity and life itself hinges upon our acceptance of the existence of God. Without God, life would not fit together. Without God, life would be an unsolvable puzzle. Without God, we would not exist; we could not even take our next breath.

The Scriptures assume the existence of God. Paul's words of affirmation leave little doubt as to his understanding of God's existence and His dealings with men: "The God who made the world and everything in it is the Lord of heaven and earth and does not live in temples built by hands. And he is not served by human hands, as if he needed anything, because he himself gives all men life and breath and everything else. From one man he made every nation of men that they should inhabit the whole earth; and he determined the times set for them and the exact places where they should live. God did this so that men would seek him and perhaps reach out for him and find him, though he is not far from each one of us. For in him we live and move and have our being" (Acts 17:24-28).

The truth of God's existence is not dependent upon our knowledge or acceptance of the fact. The Scriptures indicate that man is a fool if he says in his heart, "There is no God" (Psalm 14:1). Man can choose to ignore the facts to his own detriment.

THE TRINITY

We believe in one God, a Triune God, which means Tri-unity, God the Father, God the Son, and God the Holy Spirit. These three make up the Godhead or Trinity; three distinct personalities, yet one essence. The Trinity is probably one of the most difficult aspects of Christian doctrine to grasp and understand. It takes a theologian and a scholar to adequately describe it, although the Trinity will always remain a mystery. However, we need to have some understanding because, as we shall see later, the Trinity is intricately involved in the plan of salvation for man.

Unfortunately, our thinking is so limited to the finite that it is restricted in its capacity to even contemplate, let alone comprehend, such a divine mystery. We find it difficult to think outside of our dimension of time and space. Therefore in our attempt to explain the Trinity, we offer comparisons aligned with what we know in our natural setting.

However, although no natural illustration of the Trinity is ever adequate, some have tried to liken it to water. Water comes in three elements, liquid, ice, and vapor, yet the essence remains the same throughout. It may be inadequate as an illustration, but this has helped some people to understand the same essence existing in three different constituents.

We also talk about the three persons in the Godhead. This, too, does little to help our understanding because our concept of person is as a body with arms and legs, which occupies space; whereas God is Spirit, as are the other members of the Godhead. There are not three bodies in the Trinity, but that is how it sounds when we sing "God in three persons, blessed Trinity;" simply put, *person* is the best word we can find.

The Scriptures never actually use the word "Trinity," but its presence and existence is implied by various passages as well as the words of Jesus. At the baptism of Jesus as recorded in Mark's Gospel, we see the Trinity all present on that occasion. As Jesus was coming out of the water, the Spirit descended upon him as a dove with the Father speaking from heaven, all at the same time (Mark 1:10-11).

We are particularly drawn to John's Gospel when looking at the Trinity because of the words of Jesus, who confirms the existence of the Trinity by inference and explanation of the divine relationships within the Godhead. When Jesus talks to his disciples about the promised Holy Spirit, whom he calls "Comforter" or "Counselor," he shows how he and the Father are involved in sending the Spirit. He calls the Spirit "he" as in a person and says that he will come from the Father. Just as Jesus' ministry was to bring glory to the Father, so Jesus says that the Holy Spirit will glorify Him—that is, Jesus.

Although from Scripture we see that each member of the Godhead exercises different roles, there is no hierarchy in the Godhead. However, there seems to be some order, with the Father sending the Son, and the Holy Spirit being sent by the Father and the Son. It would appear that there is an encircling of equal love, fellowship, and unity between the

Three. During Jesus' earthly ministry, he deferred to the Father's will and authority and, at the same time, received upon himself the ministry of the Spirit of God.

In talking about this order within the Trinity and God's work on earth, George Smeaton, the late nineteenth century Free Church of Scotland theologian, gave this explanation: "As to the divine works, the Father is the source from which every operation emanates, the Son is the medium through which it is performed, and the Holy Ghost is the executive by which it is carried into effect."[3] This seems to be most plausible when we see the divine activity recorded in Scripture. Yet, even while their roles might differ, there is an extraordinary oneness and unity displayed within the Godhead.

In John's Gospel chapter 14, we find Jesus referring several times to the oneness between him and the Father. He says, "If you really knew me you would know my Father" (verse 7) and again, "Don't you believe that I am in the Father and that the Father is in me? The words I say to you are not just my own. Rather, it is the Father, living in me, who is doing his work. Believe me when I say that I am in the Father and the Father is in me" (verses 10-11). Later Jesus says, "All that belongs to the Father is mine" (John 16:15), and referring to the sending of the Holy Spirit into the world by the Father and the Son, he states, "That is why I said the Spirit will take from what is mine and make it known to you" (John 16:15). The unity in the Godhead is evident.

The relationship between Father and Son is again emphasized by Jesus in his high priestly prayer when he says "that all of them may be one, Father, just as you are in me and I am in you. May they also be in us so that the world may believe that you have sent me" (John 17:21).

Jesus clearly refers to the Trinity in Matthew 28:19 when he instructs the apostles to "make disciples of all nations, baptizing them in the name of the Father, and of the Son and of the Holy Spirit." Paul uses a similar phrase in a blessing he offers at the end of his letter when he says, "May the grace of the Lord Jesus Christ, and the love of God, and the fellowship of the Holy Spirit be with you all" (2 Corinthians 13:14).

The Trinity is seen in creation as we see plurality within the Godhead when God says, "Let us make man in our image, in our likeness" (Genesis 1:26). Later, referring to man, he says, "The man has now become like one of us, knowing good and evil" (Genesis 3:22).

Belief in the Trinity is not just an optional extra or an add-on when accepting the existence of God. It is important and necessary as each member of the Trinity is involved in God's plan of salvation for man. If the Trinity is not accepted, their individual contributions from within the Godhead cannot then be understood and acknowledged.

THE INSPIRATION OF SCRIPTURE

The third main pillar of Christianity is the inspiration of Scripture. Most religions are based upon the teachings of a man, a prophet, a spiritual guru, or a set of spiritual or philosophical principles. The basis and authority of the Christian faith is unique because its basis is twofold, the teaching of Jesus and the Holy Scriptures. Jesus came to earth as the Incarnate Living Word of God, and the Scriptures were left for us as the written Word of God. In the Gospel of John, Jesus is referred to as the *logos*, which is Greek for *Word*. We read, "The Word became flesh and lived for a while among us. We have seen his glory, the glory of the one and only Son, who came from the Father, full of grace and truth" (John 1:14).

Just as Jesus came as the Living Word of God carrying the message of salvation, so the Bible reveals that same message in written form. The Bible carries the authority and power of God because it is his Word. In the same way that Jesus spoke the Word with authority and authenticity, so the Scriptures do today. It is God speaking directly to man. Yes, it is true that the Bible was the work of man—in fact, about forty men wrote from their different backgrounds and experiences—but they wrote under the inspiration of the Holy Spirit. What does that mean? It was not dictation, but their writing was certainly guided and orchestrated by the work of God's Spirit, although each man's personality can be seen within their various writings.

Paul writing to Timothy says, "All Scripture is God-breathed and is useful for teaching, rebuking, correcting and training in righteousness" (2 Timothy 3:16). It is the divinely inspired Word of God. As such, it is infallible and carries divine authority for the practice of our faith. God, through the Holy Spirit, gave direction to its writings. When you see the order, the harmony, and the coordination throughout Scripture, penned by so many different writers over hundreds of years, it leaves little doubt that man could not have achieved this on his own. It had to be supernatural. Through the prophecies of the Old Testament, the authors foretold hundreds of events that were to take place almost a thousand years later. The New Testament records the fulfillment of those prophecies down to extraordinary detail. We see this particularly in the birth, the life, the ministry, the death, and the resurrection of Jesus.

The Bible has proved its authenticity many times over. It has been confirmed historically, geographically, archeologically, prophetically and, of course, spiritually. It is now thought that most of the books of the New Testament were written no later than 80 AD. That is less than fifty years from the death of Christ, and with the existence today of at least 24,000 total or partial manuscripts of the New Testament, this is ample literary proof of its authenticity. Few, if any, manuscripts in the literary world can compare with such a record.

As the Word of God, the Scriptures hold an inherent power for changing lives. As we find written earlier in that passage quoted in 2 Timothy 3:15, "You have known the holy Scriptures, which are able to make you wise for salvation through faith in Christ Jesus." This is also expressed in Hebrews 4:12, where we read, "For the word of God is living and active. Sharper than any double-edged sword, it penetrates even to dividing soul and spirit, joints and marrow; it judges the thoughts and attitudes of the heart." The Bible is not just a collection of books but is the Word of God which searches the hearts of men and exposes the hidden secrets, both good and bad. God's Word brings man to account. That same Scripture goes on to say, "Nothing in all creation is hidden from God's sight. Everything is uncovered and laid bare before the eyes of him to whom we must give an account" (Hebrews 4:13).

David Suchet, the well-known British actor, indicates that he came to faith in Christ simply by reading the New Testament. There are innumerable similar testimonies of those who have found faith in Jesus Christ simply by reading the Scriptures. The divine inspiration of Scripture is confirmed by the very fact that it is powerful and life-changing. We should not be surprised that the Bible remains a best seller every year, outselling other books by the millions. If it were included on the top-seller list, there would rarely be a week that it did not appear there. It is the guidebook, the standard, the measure (and if you want to call it a rulebook, then it is that also) to every believer.

As Christians, we must revere it for what it is—the very Word of God. Because it is inspired, it speaks to us today. The message within is revealed to us and applied by the Spirit of God. It brings comfort, strength, direction, and instruction as we read, listen, and obey. There is no other book in the world to compare with the Bible, both in its divine origin and its spiritual ministry in changing the lives of millions of people. The Scriptures are like a tapestry depicting God's relationship with man.

So there you have it: the three main pillars of the Christian faith. Remove any one of them and the faith will collapse. We now move from acknowledging the existence of God, the Trinity, and the inspiration of Scripture into more detailed questions of our faith. As all faiths start with God, it is not unreasonable to ask the question, "Who is God?"

but in our context, it would be more appropriate to ask, "Who is the Christian's God?" This we can know through the pages of Scripture. Thus, we move forward to tackle just such a question.

✖

QUESTIONS FOR GROUP STUDY
WHAT ARE THE PILLARS OF CHRISTIANITY?

Reading: Hebrews 11:1-6

1. Can we ever prove the existence of God to a non-believer?

2. How much does faith play into accepting this doctrine?

3. Describe the different functions of each member of the Trinity.

4. Is it essential that we believe in the Trinity? If so, why?

5. What evidence do we have for the authenticity of the Scriptures?

6. Share a time or experience when the Scriptures proved real to you and made a difference in your life.

3

WHO IS GOD THE FATHER?

"You will know that I am the Lord your God."
EXODUS 16:12

Shirley was a teenager who lived with her mother and father in a small town in the north of England. Unfortunately, both she and her mother suffered mental and physical abuse from the father. As far back as Shirley could remember, her father had a nasty temper, and it took very little to upset him and send him into a rage and subsequent abusive action. Shortly after the father arrived home from work was one of the worst times of the day. It was then when he was most susceptible to his irate and unreasonable outbursts. Shirley and her mother spent the evenings in an unnatural silence. It was like walking on eggshells. It was a relief when the father went off to the local drinking establishment, although they dreaded his return home.

Both mother and daughter tolerated this treatment for years. In fact, Shirley came to accept this life and behavior as normal, until one day her mother had to go to hospital for ten days, and her father agreed that Shirley could stay with a school friend named Catherine. What she experienced at Catherine's house took her by surprise. She discovered there a happy family where mother and the children were well treated and the father was genuinely courteous and loving. She suddenly began to compare her own home life and see her father for what he really was—a tyrant. Upon her return home, she shared this discovery with her mother, who simply dismissed the information with "Life is what it is and little can be done about it." So life continued on the same; although Shirley left the home as soon as was possible, the negative impressions of her father and the emotional turmoil remained with her for many years.

I tell you this story of Shirley because it is not uncommon for the view we hold of our earthly father to be transferred to God the Father. For many, that earthly father is the only example they have of a father; if that view is negative, then difficulties arise in coming to understand a God of love and compassion. They can readily accept a God of wrath and anger but have great difficulty in identifying with a Father who cares. There are those who feel that such a scenario should drive a person in the opposite direction—causing them to readily accept the concept of a God of love—but I believe that tends to be the exception. There is, of course, no perfect human example of the character of God. No human father, however good, can be the equal of God the Father.

God is our Father, full of love and compassion. He cares for us as his children. He disciplines us as his children. He longs for our response to him as Father. He watches over us constantly. He is ever present, fulfilling his promise that "Never will I leave you; never will I forsake you" (Hebrews 13:5).

A story is told of a small girl in school who drew a picture. When asked by the teacher what she was drawing, she answered, "I am drawing a picture of God."

"But," replied the teacher, "nobody has seen God, so nobody knows what God looks like."

"No, but they will when I have finished my picture," said the little girl.

That's a cute story, but the teacher is right. No man has seen God and lived. In fact, God gave several warnings in Scripture concerning the dangers of man being in his presence. Even the high priest who entered the Holy of Holies to offer sacrifices had to be properly prepared to go into the very presence of God.

A Gallup poll taken a few years ago indicated that 97% of Americans believed in God. One wonders what kind of a God would command such a high response. For many it would be a God of personal creation, of one's own imagination. For some it would be the summation of a collection of bits and pieces received from various sources throughout life. It is not uncommon for people to take a little information from their childhood memories, from parents, from early days at church, and maybe add a large contribution from the media, and formulate a concept of God. It is usually a concept which is comfortable and calls for little or no accountability. Christians, too, can be guilty of the same exercise.

Several years ago I read the following revealing—even startling— statement: "If we worship any concept of God which is non-biblical, then we worship an idol." It sounds harsh, but it is true because any other concept would be a god of our own imagination. There is only one God. All other gods exist only in the minds of men. Isaiah made this clear when he uttered the very words of God, "This is what the Lord says—Israel's King and Redeemer, the Lord Almighty: I am the first and I am the last; apart from me there is no God" (Isaiah 44:6).

What comes to mind when you think of God? If you were asked to describe your concept of God, what would you say? Most of us would struggle to find adequate words to verbalize our thinking. Yet probably all of us, except maybe an avowed atheist, have some kind of a mental image of God. The man in the street has a view. People in the pew have a view. The view we have may be vague because it is hard for us to think of a non-physical God, which of course is necessary as God is Spirit. Yet our concept of God is important because it determines our belief system. It also forms the basis for our worldview.

From one of Charles Spurgeon's sermons come these words: "The highest science, the loftiest speculation, the mightiest philosophy which can ever engage the attention of a child of God is the name, the nature, the person, the work, the doings, and the existence of the great God whom he calls as Father."[1] We can do no better than engage ourselves in just such a study. Yet it is presumptuous to even think, or imply, that any one of us might have the audacity to attempt to adequately describe God. We can only look at the Scriptures to see how God is mirrored in those sacred pages.

God is the source of all. He created life and sustains life. Without him, life would be an unsolvable puzzle. Without him, we could not exist. God is the foundation of all doctrine; therefore, any study of the Christian faith must first seek to understand who God is and look at his nature and his attributes. Then we can better understand our relationship to him.

We all have preconceived ideas of God, but we must ask the question, "What is the biblical concept of God?" It is impossible for any of us to comprehend the magnificence, the majesty, and the transcendence of God. We, in our finite humanness, can only recognize him by his divine nature and characteristics.

GOD IS SPIRIT

In John chapter four, we read about Jesus talking to the Samaritan woman at the well. In response to her question regarding worship, Jesus explained that the time was coming when man's worship of God would not be restricted to any one place but would be in their hearts and minds. Also, because God is Spirit, those who worship him must do so in spirit and truth. Jesus declared that God is Spirit, which means that God is a personal, non-physical being.

Being Spirit means that, although God is invisible, he is everywhere. He is omnipresent—everywhere at the same time. In Psalm 139, David asked the question, "Where can I go from your Spirit?" He indicates that there is no place on earth where God is not. God is not restricted to any one place at any one time. Our omnipresent God is free from any limitation. He is boundless. There are no boundaries to which God can be subjected.

We are never out of God's sight, a fact which might be disturbing for some but for the believer is comforting and assuring. It means that God is fully present with believers the world over—thus he hears and answers thousands of prayers at the same time. This is how he can divinely intervene in personal lives and situations all over the globe at the same time.

Some have asked the question, "How big is God?" The answer to that is that he fills the universe with his presence. That is how big he is. Yet Jesus came as the full and complete expression of the Father. In John 1:18, we read that Jesus made the invisible visible. Jesus said, "If you have seen me, you have seen the Father." Jesus says that he and the Father are one—a confirmation of Jesus' presence in the Trinity.

GOD IS INFINITE

As humans, we are finite. We have a beginning and an end and are restricted to the dimensions of time and space. That is not so with God. God is infinite and lives in infinity. But what is infinity? Hold a coin in your hand and ask yourself where the edge begins and ends. Draw a circle and ask yourself the same question: "Where is the beginning and the end of the circle?" These are illustrations of infinity: there is no beginning, and there is no end. That's why God says in Revelation 1:8, "I am the Alpha and the Omega, ... who is, and who was, and who is to come, the Almighty." God is saying that he is the beginning and the end.

God himself had no beginning. God told Moses, "I am that I am." The "I am" is the holy supreme title for God, who is an ever present, self-existent being who had no beginning; he always was. God is not restricted to the dimensions of time and space because God exists in timelessness. He was not self created. God is self-existent; he always existed. There never was a time when God was not. He existed in eternity. He is self-sufficient, independent. He is the source of all life. Man would not exist if God did not exist, clarified nicely by R.C.Sproul with this phrase, "We are, because he is."[2]

Because God is infinite, he is omniscient—which means he knows everything. We can only see in the present. We can remember the past and anticipate the future, but because God is outside our dimension, he knows the beginning and the end. He sees the beginning of time and the end of time at the same time. He has already been there. There is no difference for God between the past, the present, and the future. All time and everything is present with God. This is why the book of Revelation can tell us that Christ was slain before the foundation of the world, because in God it had already taken place.

What spiritual benefit is this to us? God knows what you will think tomorrow. God knows what you will go through next month, next year, or the coming years. God holds tomorrow in his hands. We can live with comfort and confidence in the knowledge that if we are God's children, part of his family, then whatever might be ahead for us, our Father has already been there.

GOD IS CREATOR

Genesis 1:1 shows us that God, as Creator, is the source of all being. He is the source of all life, of everything living, plants, animals, and humans. What's more, he sustains that life day by day. We read in Acts that "he himself gives all men life and breath and everything else." Then again in the same passage, "In him we live and move and have our being" (Acts 17:28). He is our source of life. We exist by his power and continue to exist because of God's grace and permission.

The Psalmist says, "The heavens declare the glory of God, the skies proclaim the work of his hands" (Psalm 19:1). As Creator, God displays his omnipotence, which means his power. He is almighty and all powerful. He created the world out of nothing. Just try to comprehend that phrase. God spoke and it happened! Consider the expanse and the vastness of the universe, or the detailed complexity of the human body. God made it all from nothing. We can think of no greater power!

If you do any reading on the universe, you quickly realize the remarkable coordination and just how much everything fits together. You learn how the earth, the planets, the moon, the sun, and the stars are all in perfect symmetry. They are not where they are because of an accident of nature. They have been specifically placed to allow life on Earth. The details and fine tuning of the universe is mind-boggling. For instance, just a two-percent change in the distance of the sun from Earth would render the Earth uninhabitable. If the sun were closer, we would burn up; if further away, it would be too cold for life to exist. This special placement of the Earth, the moon, the planets, and the sun attests to our great Creator. Even the rotation of the Earth is critical. If it was slower and we had a thirty-six hour day, the light side would overheat, while the dark side would freeze.

Hugh Ross, in his book *The Creator of the Cosmos*, talks extensively about how a specific place in the universe was chosen for the Earth, a place where life could be sustained. He says, "If divine design is essential to explain the properties of simpler systems such as the universe, our galaxy, and the solar system, then God's involvement is even more essential to explain systems as complex as organisms, including human beings."[3] The intricate nature of our bodies and how the various systems within the body are so perfectly synergized is astounding. No computer can be constructed to match the complexity of the human brain.

Because of all the evidence of God's handiwork, we as believers exercise our faith in the truth of God's intervention. This is confirmed in Hebrews, where it says that "By faith we understand that the universe was formed at God's command, so that what is seen was not made out of what was visible" (Hebrews 11:3). God created the world by the power of his word. He created the world from nothing—a fact now attested to by many scientists as they turn the clock of the universe back to zero. The earth was formed from outside of itself. The Maker had to be outside of the universe.

Self-proclaimed agnostic Robert Jastrow, an astrophysicist, makes a delightful statement in his book, *God and the Astronomers.* He says, "For the scientist who has lived by his faith in the power of reason, the story ends like a bad dream. He has scaled the mountains of ignorance; he is about to conquer the highest peak, as he pulls himself over the final rock, he is greeted by a band of theologians who have been sitting there for centuries."[4]

God has revealed himself through Creation, as seen in Romans chapter one. The Creation shows God's hand through its design, its detailed complexity, and its order. As Creator God rules over all, he is Lord of all Creation. God revealed himself to man, but man generally has chosen not to accept the evidence and chooses not to believe—both to his discredit and his downfall.

GOD IS IMMUTABLE

Immutable simply means unchangeable. Man over time is in constant change. We are all too aware of the changes within our bodies, usually not for the better. Tragically, our cells can mutate, which can then lead to serious illness. There are changes within our minds. We even change in character as we grow and mature. Everything about us is changeable because of our humanness.

God is immutable. Every aspect of him is unchangeable. He does not develop, improve, or advance with years. As if confirming this fact, we read, "In the beginning you laid the foundations of the earth, and the heavens are the work of your hands. They will perish but you remain… they will be discarded but you remain the same, your years will never end" (Psalm 102:25-27). In fact, there is no such thing as time with God.

God cannot change. He says in Malachi 3:6, "I the Lord do not change." His character never changes. All his attributes are immutable. This means his holiness, his justice, his love, his compassion, his goodness, his righteousness, all remain constant. His plan and purpose for man and for the church remain the same. As Jesus is part of the Godhead, the Scriptures also refer to his immutability in Hebrews 13:8 where it states, "Jesus Christ is the same yesterday, and today and forever." God's Word never changes. God's Word is eternal. Referring to God, the Psalmist says, "Long ago I learned from your statutes that you established them to last forever" (Psalm 119:152).

My wife and I are very blessed to have an apartment overlooking the water facing west. We see some magnificent sunsets. We also see the effect of the clouds as they move across the water. The clouds create dark areas on the water and cause the water to appear in constant change, both in color and shade. This reminds us of the words of James in his epistle. "Every good and perfect gift is from above, coming down from the Father of heavenly lights, who does not change like shifting shadows" (James 1:17). There are no shadows with God. His presence only brings light. God is eternally constant. He is, and will always be, immutable, unchangeable in all his ways.

GOD IS HOLY

If you were asked to describe God in your own words, the word "holy" would probably be one of the first words of description. A number of times in the Bible, God places a strong emphasis upon his holiness. In Leviticus 20:26, God declares that he is holy and expects his children to be the same. He says, "You are to be holy to me because I, the Lord, am holy, and I have set you apart from the nations to be my own."

The word "holy" is not easy to understand. The primary meaning is *to be separate, to be set apart* as indicated by the Scripture text above. There are many references in Scripture where places or things are called holy because they have been set apart for God. We read about the holy vessels in the temple, holy ground, holy city, holy Ark, holy covenant, holy Word, holy of holies, and many more examples. These have all been set apart for God. But this principle of separation also applies to God himself. He is separate, he is different, "there is none like him," says the Scripture. Some writers describe God as being "other" because there are no adequate words to describe his uniqueness.

This aspect of God's divine nature is all encompassing. His holiness transcends everything. His Spirit is holy, he is infinitely holy, and his creation displays his holiness. His whole character is holiness personified. When we come into the presence of God, we are in the presence of the holy. The realization of that holiness should fill us with awe and respect.

The one aspect of God's holiness that is more commonly recognized is the characteristic of purity. God cannot sin. No moral blemish, no defect, no sin can exist within God's presence. No sin can ever taint his holiness. Such is the divine nature and character of God. As with many other aspects of God, the awesomeness of God's holiness goes beyond our comprehension.

Yet we read in Peter's epistle that God says to his children, "Be ye holy for I am holy" (1 Peter 1:16). "Is that even possible?" we might ask. The good news is that if we are in the family of God, then we are already holy by position because we are covered by the righteousness of Christ, and as Christ is holy, so we too are deemed holy. That is how God looks at us—through the righteousness of Christ. We are already "set apart" to serve God. But we are called to be practically holy—holy in our behavior, in our attitudes, in our language, and in our daily Christian walk. This is why the Christian is indwelt by the Holy Spirit of God: to enable him to walk in step with the Spirit and do those things which are pleasing to God. We have a responsibility to seek to attain the purity of holiness—this is holiness in practice.

GOD IS JUST

Early in the Scriptures we find God threatening to destroy the city of Sodom because of the people's wickedness. But Abraham pleads with God regarding the lives of the righteous who might live in Sodom. Abraham asks God if he would spare the city for the sake of fifty righteous people and makes a statement to God about God as Judge. He says, "Will not the Judge of all the earth do right?" (Genesis 18:25). In other words, will you not be just in your dealings with these people? God not only agrees to save the city for fifty righteous people but agrees not to destroy the city if Abraham can find ten righteous people. Abraham's view of a just God was vindicated. He knew that God, being true to his Being, would act righteously in the issuance of divine justice.

The dictionary definition of just is "morally right or fair." This is the description of the justice of God. The Scripture teaches that he is just and the justifier. As a just God, he must fulfill his justice. He is just and true. To be true to his character means being just. God cannot be something he is not; therefore, as a just God, he must fulfill his justice. Consequently, he cannot overlook sin—it would be against his very nature. But the fulfillment of his justice is with absolute fairness. God always acts according to his righteous nature. It is impossible for him to be anything else. He is morally right, morally perfect, and thus morally just and fair.

Because of God's omniscience, he is totally aware of every aspect of every situation. Because of this, he is perfectly just. There is never a question of injustice, of wrongful accusation, or of unfair punishment. It is good for us to be reminded that Jesus was unfairly accused and wrongfully punished, and he did it willingly for us. Jesus suffered the pain of God's justice so that we might be recipients of God's love and grace.

How often have we been unjustly accused of wrong doing, misunderstood, or misrepresented? We can tolerate being justly accused when we are guilty, but to be falsely accused is painful and emotionally disturbing. Yet God knows the truth. Maybe he alone knows the whole truth. We can be assured of proper vindication. As our Father is also a just God, he can right wrongs, he can bring good out of evil, and he can bring justice into any situation. But more importantly, he is the justifier, which means he brings spiritual justification into our lives through the atonement made for us through Jesus on the cross—but more about that later.

GOD IS LOVE

We purposely follow the aspect of God's justice with the fact that God is love. These two aspects of God's character need to be recognized together because when they get separated, it can lead to an imbalanced and unhealthy spiritual viewpoint. People want a comfortable concept of God, but often without including justice. This leads to the conception of a one-sided God. They desire to have a God who is only love and conveniently forget that God is just, and his very holiness demands justice. Some say, "A God who brings judgment on man is not the God I know. The God I know is loving, gentle, and forgiving." That is an imbalanced view of God and the Scriptures.

Man sinned and rebelled against a holy God. God cannot overlook sin; otherwise, he would not be just. He would not be true to his nature. So out of his holiness came his wrath, which demanded satisfaction. Thus every man was condemned, and the death sentence was passed upon all. But God, who is also perfect love, "so loved the world that he gave his one and only son" to receive the death sentence in place of man. Man no longer needs to live under condemnation and live with the sentence of death upon him. God provided the solution. God placed our punishment upon Christ, who died in our place.

So the justice of God and the love of God met at Calvary. We see that this is where God demonstrated the depth of his love for us, while at the same time satisfying the need to fulfill his own justice against sin. Thus, through the Cross, we receive the forgiveness of sin and become recipients of God's grace, compassion, love, and mercy.

"God is love," says John (1 John 4:8), but what does that mean? His very being is love. His nature is love. He exudes love. All love which exists emanates from God. He is the source of love. His love is unconditional. His love is poured into the life of the believer. There is nothing we can do to increase that love. His love is already perfect. God does not love us because we love him. It is because he first loved us that we are able to respond in love to him. How incredible to find that we can never be separated from that love. Paul says, "For I am convinced that neither death nor life, neither angels nor demons, neither the present or the future, nor any powers, neither height nor depth, nor anything else in all creation, will be able to separate us from the love of God that is in Christ Jesus our Lord" (Romans 8:38-39). God's love is unfathomable and is as constant as his nature.

GOD IS SOVEREIGN

As Creator, God is sovereign. He made everything; therefore, he is over everything and rules everything. His sovereignty means that he rules over all and is in control. As sovereign, he is the supreme ruler with supreme power. His plans and purposes cannot be thwarted.

The Scriptures ask the rhetorical question several times, "Is anything too hard for the Lord?" and of course, the answer is no. There is nothing too hard for God to accomplish. There is no situation beyond his capacity to intervene, if he so chooses. In my earlier book, *"If We Only Knew... Remarkable True Stories of God's Intervention,"* I related many stories of God's intervention in people's lives. They were stories of financial provision, of protection under persecution and imprisonment, of God providing and multiplying provisions, and many other situations where God directly intervened and orchestrated situations for the benefit of the recipients but also for his glory. The book is a testimony to the working of God's sovereignty.

Daniel, who was unjustly punished for his faithfulness to God, expresses little doubt about God being in control when he says, "Praise be to the name of God forever and ever; wisdom and power are his. He changes times and seasons; he sets up kings and disposes them. He gives wisdom to the wise and knowledge to the discerning. He reveals deep and hidden things; he knows what lies in darkness, and light dwells in him" (Daniel 2:20-22). Knowing God is sovereign and in total control should bring comfort to all Christians.

When we look at life in the light of God's sovereignty, we must come to the conclusion that all that happens to us is for his glory. Whether the events are good or bad, it must ultimately be for our spiritual betterment and for furthering the purpose and plan of God our Father.

WHO IS GOD THE FATHER?

If we, in our humanness, could just catch a glimpse of God in all his majesty and supremacy, we would do well. As we contemplate God as Spirit, infinite, eternal, and sovereign from whom emanates holiness, love, and justice, it is no small privilege that we can call him Father. Such an intimate privilege comes from our being called and accepted within the family of God. Such a special relationship is open to all but, regrettably, it is ignored by many. God, who is all powerful, all knowing, ever present, and rules over all, allows us to be recipients of his love, his mercy, his compassion, and his grace. This is the God we serve. This is God the Father.

QUESTIONS FOR GROUP STUDY
WHO IS GOD THE FATHER?

Reading: John 17:1-19

1. What would you say is the common view of God in the world?

2. What would you say is the Christian's common concept of God?

3. What do you understand about the sovereignty of God?

4. Which of God's characteristics brings you comfort? Are there any that cause you concern?

5. How do we equate the wrath of God with the love of God?

6. How do we handle the fact that God, who is so supreme, so majestic, and so high above all, takes a personal interest in each of us? Can we truly grasp the truth of that?

4

WHO IS GOD THE SON?

"Grace and truth came through Jesus Christ."
JOHN 1:17

Do you remember the days when it was advised that you not discuss religion and politics in the work place? It was feared that discussion might turn into heated arguments and result in severed or damaged relationships. Yet the advice was not always observed and, on those occasions, it was interesting to hear the comments on religion and particularly on the identity of Jesus. How common it was to hear "he was a good man," "he was a good moral teacher," or the other one, "he was a good man who left us a great example of how to live." Some would concede that there was more to it, that "he was a prophet." Even some non-Christian religions adopt that position, but to the Christian, Jesus was and is the Son of God.

The Scriptures show us that Jesus is the one and only Son of God, "begotten of the Father," not created as were the angels. Christ is divine. He is the second person of the Trinity. He is part of the Godhead, and as such, embodies all the attributes of God. The attributes and characteristics of the Father are identical in the Son because "He and the Father are one" as indicated by Jesus' prayer in John 17.

We can probably best answer the question, "Who is the Son of God?" by looking at the life of Jesus. What he did was an expression of who he is. He demonstrated his identity as God and as man.

HIS INCARNATION

It was 700 years prior to his birth that the prophets predicted his coming, along with the location and the method of his birth. Can you think of a more strange prediction than "a virgin shall conceive and bring forth a son," when such an event had never occurred previously in history? The prophecy had to be of divine origin.

When we talk about the lives of great men of history such as Churchill or Einstein, we say they were "born" on a specific date, but when we talk about Jesus, we speak differently. Although we say he was born in Bethlehem, we more commonly say he "came" to earth. This plainly implies that he previously existed—that he "was" before he came here.

In chapter one of John's Gospel, we have the well-known portion of Scripture that indicates the pre-existence of Christ. We read, "In the beginning was the Word, and the Word was with God, and the Word was God. He was with God in the beginning" (John 1:1). The Word here refers to Christ, the *Logos*. He was the living Word of God. It clearly states that Jesus was with God from the beginning and that he was God; thus our earlier reference to him having all the attributes and characteristics of God the Father. Paul took the same view in talking about Christ Jesus when he stated, "Who, being in very nature God, did not consider equality with God something to be grasped, but made himself nothing, taking the very nature of a servant, being made in human likeness." Here we see Christ recognized as God and co-equal with the Father.

Christ's presence in the Godhead before the foundation of the world is confirmed by Christ's involvement in Creation, related for us in Colossians 1:15-17, where we read, "He is the image of the invisible God, the firstborn over all creation. For by him all things were created: things in heaven and on earth, visible and invisible....all things were created by him and for him. He is before all things, and in him all things hold together."

To recognize the deity of Jesus is critical to the Christian faith. If Jesus was not divine, then the Cross and the death of Christ become redundant. John emphasizes that his Gospel was written so that "you may believe that Jesus is the Christ, the Son of God" (John 20:31). The uniqueness of Christianity is the uniqueness of Christ.

Think for a moment about the miracle of the virgin birth. It could only have been brought about with God's intervention. We read in Galatians 4:4 these words: "When the time was fully come, God sent his son, born of a woman." The birth through Mary was crucial so that Christ was authentically human, but the virgin birth was also essential. Being conceived by the Holy Spirit was not the time when Jesus began to exist. He already existed within the Godhead prior to Creation; thus it was impossible for him to have been tainted with the sin of Adam. Jesus himself says, "...before Abraham was born, I am!"(John 8:38), which confirms his preincarnate existence.

Conceived by the Holy Spirit, Jesus remained morally and spiritually perfect. He could not be born of man; otherwise, he would not have been sinless. He would have been born under the bondage of sin with the guilt of sin, and he too would have stood in need of the grace of God. However, it was not so. His birth was supernatural and miraculous. The virgin birth was a sign of Christ's deity, his divine power, his divine purity, his position in the Godhead. It identified him as the Christ, the Messiah, and the Anointed One.

John succinctly describes this as "The Word became flesh and made his dwelling among us" (John 1:14). This was the incarnation which was birthed in the heart of God and demonstrated his goodness, his love, and his grace toward us. This was the embodiment of God in Christ. This was God providing the solution to man's dilemma—providing the answer to man's sinful condition and his self-imposed condemnation. However, all of this was contingent upon the deity of Christ. The plan of God would have been ineffectual if Christ had not been the Son of God, pre-existent and eternal.

Because Jesus spoke about the special relationship he had with the Father, the Jews sought to kill him. To them, he was making blasphemous statements about his identity. In John 20:17, just before his ascension, Jesus said, "I am returning to my Father and your father, to my God and your God." The fact that he was returning indicates that he was there previously.

It was Isaiah the prophet who, while prophesying regarding the incarnation, said that Jesus would be called "Wonderful Counselor, Mighty God, Everlasting Father, Prince of Peace," identifying him directly with the other members of the Trinity. It was also Isaiah who stated, "The virgin will be with child and will give birth to a son, and will call him Immanuel" (Isaiah 7:14). The title simply means "God with us," which is exactly what happened. We see God coming down to man. This was God making the move himself to bring peace and reconciliation to man's broken relationship with him. It was he who sent Jesus to break through into our time, our space, and our history to bring us salvation. The interesting aspect here is that if Jesus had not been Immanuel, then he could not have been Jesus. Jesus means "Savior," and he could not have been Savior without being God!

As we begin to grasp the real reason and truth behind the incarnation, we come to recognize that the ultimate purpose of the incarnation was the crucifixion. For Christ, the road to Calvary began at Bethlehem. There are eight words regarding the birth of Jesus that were given to Joseph by the angel. When the angel instructed Joseph to call the baby, "Jesus," he added, "for he shall save his people from their sin." This is the center, this is the core of the miracle: Christ bringing forgiveness and salvation to man. This was the good news of great joy about which the angels sang. The cross was not the result of the cradle; it was the purpose.

HIS MINISTRY

Christ's three years of ministry were packed with miracles and meeting the needs of people. He displayed compassion, mercy, grace, and love, yet he was grossly misunderstood and mistreated. He showed authority in his teaching and knowledge. People were amazed. The religious rulers of the day were perplexed, confused, angry, indignant, and jealous. They felt their authority and positions of power were threatened and undermined. Consequently, they did all they could to kill Jesus.

Immediately following his baptism by John the Baptist, Jesus was anointed and filled with the Spirit in preparation for his ministry and then led by the Spirit into the wilderness. He spent the next forty days alone in the wilderness withstanding the temptations of Satan. His ministry commenced with opposition and continued that way for three years. He came with a message of salvation to the Jews, but they rejected the message. They refused to acknowledge him as the Messiah. John says, "He came to that which was his own, but his own did not receive him" (John 1:11).

During his ministry, Jesus showed the human characteristics of tiredness and thirst when he needed to rest and drink. He showed his anger or righteous indignation against the money-changers who were using the temple to exploit people and make money fraudulently. He showed emotion as he wept at the grave of Lazarus. He displayed his compassion to the thousands of people whom he saw as sheep without a shepherd. He exuded love and understanding to those who needed his healing touch and who needed to know his forgiveness. Although meek in attitude, he was strong when it came to confronting the Pharisees and Sadducees and forcing them to face the truth.

The writer of the book of Hebrews gives the reason for Jesus taking on flesh and experiencing humanity as he did. He states, "For this reason he had to be made like his brothers in every way, in order that he might become a merciful and faithful high priest in service to God, and that he might make atonement for the sins of the people. Because he himself suffered when he was tempted, he is able to help those who are being tempted" (Hebrews 2:17-18). Then, talking about Christ as our high priest, he goes on, "But we do not have a high priest who is unable to sympathize with our weaknesses, but we have one who has been tempted in every way, just as we are—yet was without sin" (Hebrews 4:15). His sinless life was necessary to atone as the supreme sacrifice for our sin.

Although showing some of the limitations of the flesh, Christ never gave up the divine nature of the Godhead. He came out of the Godhead to take the role of a servant to identify with man. Jesus humbled himself to do the will of his Father. As was recorded about him in Philippians, "And being found in appearance as a man, he humbled himself and became obedient to death—even death on a cross!" (Philippians 2:8). It was there that he died in our place as only he could, but all the while, he remained fully God and fully human.

Some have asked why Jesus is referred to as Son when there is equality within the Godhead. The best explanation I have ever seen comes from the book *Knowing God* by J.I. Packer. It states, "It is the nature of the second person of the Trinity to acknowledge the authority and submit to the good pleasure of the first. That is why he declares himself to be the Son and the first person to be the Father. Though co-equal with the Father in eternity, power, and glory, it is natural for him to play the Son's part and to find all his joy in doing his Father's will, just as it is natural to the first person of the Trinity to plan and initiate the works of the Godhead and natural to the third person to proceed from the Father and the Son to do their joint bidding.

Thus the obedience of the God-Man to the Father while he was on earth was not a new relationship between the Son and the Father, but the continuation in time of the eternal relationship between the Son and the Father in heaven. As in heaven, so on earth, the Son was utterly dependent upon the Father's will."[1]

This we plainly see in the earthly mission of Jesus. He was here to fulfill the will of his Father. This he reiterated time and again throughout his earthly ministry. Even at the age of twelve, he was in the temple displaying extraordinary understanding in the presence of the teachers and indicating then to his parents that "he had to be about his Father's business." He made it abundantly clear that he had been sent by the Father to fulfill his purpose and plan. Jesus said, "For I seek not to please myself but him who sent me" (John 5:30). He then further said, "For the very work that the Father has given me to finish, and which I am doing, testifies that the Father has sent me" (John 5:36). In confirming his identity and his purpose, Jesus said, "When you have lifted up the Son of Man, then you will know who I am and that I do nothing on my own but speak just what the Father has taught me. The one who sent me is with me; he has not left me alone, for I always do what pleases him" (John 8:28-29).

The uniqueness of Christ is reflected in the uniqueness of Christianity. As opposed to human teachers, prophets, or gurus, Jesus was divine. This is his distinction: he is God, and his deity was seen in every aspect of his life and ministry.

HIS DEATH

Just as his birth was prophesied, so was his death. A thread runs throughout the Old Testament that points to the coming Messiah and the ultimate sacrifice he would make by the offering of himself. In Isaiah chapter fifty-three, we read familiar words which portray his trial, his suffering, and his death. It states that "he was led like a lamb to the slaughter, and as a sheep before her shearers is silent, so he did not open his mouth" (verse 7). His opposition was described with these words: "He was despised and rejected by men, a man of sorrows, and familiar with suffering" (verse 3). Then further on we read, "But he was pierced for our transgressions, he was crushed for our iniquities; the punishment that brought us peace was upon him" (verse 5). The chapter concludes with "he poured out his life unto death and was numbered with the transgressors. For he bore the sin of many, and made intercession for the transgressors" (verse 12). All this, stated hundreds of years prior to the death of Jesus.

Jesus was born to die. From the outset of his incarnation, his mission was to give his life as a sacrifice for sin. The road of his life pointed one way—to the Cross. As we have already seen, his purpose was to fulfill the will of his Father, and that will was for Jesus to be an offering and an atonement for the sins of mankind.

Jesus' death was significant because of who he was. If Jesus had simply been another martyr dying for a cause, his act of dying may have gone down in history books, but it would be no more than a recorded event. It was because he was the Son of God that his death was so extraordinary. Look at the events or circumstances of the day which surrounded the crucifixion. The sky became black from noon until three in the afternoon. There was an incredible earthquake. People were afraid. One soldier declared, "Surely this was the Son of God." The veil in the temple was severed from top to bottom at the same time. This veil was a six-inch-thick curtain that separated the Holy of Holies with its altar from other parts of the temple, because it was a place of sacredness and the presence of God. The significance of the torn curtain was that Jesus, because of his deity and through his death, had nullified the need for further sacrifice. He had become the supreme sacrifice to cover all the sin of mankind—past, present, and future. Through Christ's declaration on the cross, "It is finished," he indicated that his earthly mission had been completed, achieved because he was divine. His deity was beyond question.

In our humanity we might think of his death as incomprehensible, not fully understanding why he had to die the worst possible death known to man at that time. In the natural, man would look at the cross as a defeat. Even his disciples were looking for Christ to set up his own kingdom and to overthrow the reigning authorities. However, this did not occur and upon his arrest, they scattered, seeking to avoid any identification with him. But Jesus' death was far from a defeat; it was a victory—a spiritual victory. It was a victory over sin, over the power of Satan, and over death. This was confirmed three days later by the resurrection.

The death of Christ is the pinnacle and center of the Christian faith. In fact, it could be considered to be the center of history. If there had been no death of Christ, no Calvary, there would be no salvation for mankind.

HIS RESURRECTION

The resurrection of Jesus has probably received the biggest onslaught to disprove its authenticity than any other event in history. Philosophers, scholars, scientists, and historians have made immense efforts to explain away the fact of Christ's resurrection. However, they found the evidence so overwhelming that it resulted in a number of them writing books and papers, outlining their discoveries, and confirming the event. Frank Morison was one of those men. He set out to disprove the resurrection. He finished his research by writing the book *Who Moved the Stone*, wholeheartedly endorsing—and confirming—the facts of the resurrection.

A well-known professor of Classics at Auckland University in New Zealand, E.M. Blaiklock, is quoted as saying, "I claim to be an historian. My approach to Classics is historical. And I tell you that the evidence for the life, the death, and the resurrection of Christ is better authenticated than most of the facts of ancient history..."[2]

There have been all kinds of theories put forward to discount the truth of the resurrection, from the fact that Jesus did not die on the cross, to the disciples stealing the body to falsely indicate a resurrection. But the facts show up these theories for what they were—lies. The Roman soldiers would have confirmed that Jesus was dead; in fact, they pierced him with a sword to ensure he was dead. Then it was Pilate who gave instructions to seal the tomb, which was done with a large stone. To break the seal would have been a criminal offence against the authorities, a crime punishable by death. Guards were also set at the entrance.

Yet on the morning of the third day, the seal had been broken, the stone had been rolled away, and the guards had fled. The body of Jesus was no longer there, but the grave clothes—the linen garments in which he had been buried—were neatly left where he had lain. Women were first to arrive at the tomb—they could not have moved the stone. A fabricated story at the time was that the body of Jesus had been stolen, but guards had been placed earlier at the entrance to the tomb to prevent just such an occurrence.

One of the major, distinct aspects of Christianity lies within the event of the resurrection. There is no other faith or religion that can claim resurrection for its leader. All other founders, leaders, prophets, and gurus have come and gone. Jesus alone rose from the dead just as he predicted and announced to his disciples. At the empty tomb, two angels appeared and asked the women, "Why do you look for the living among the dead? He is not here; he has risen! Remember how he told you, while he was still with you in Galilee: The Son of Man must be delivered into the hands of sinful men, be crucified and on the third day be raised again" (Luke 24:5-7). Through his resurrection, Christ's earthly mission was truly completed. All that remained was his ascension.

For forty days following the resurrection, Jesus appeared to many people—sometimes two or three or a small group. Paul says that at one time he appeared to 500 people all at once, many of whom would have still been around to support what Paul was saying regarding the truth of the resurrection. Witnesses to Jesus' appearances were numerous. The disciples became bolder in their preaching and presentation of the gospel. As time went by, their attitudes confirmed the resurrection because they would have been subject to ridicule, to persecutions, to beatings, and then death by martyrdom. If the resurrection had not been a reality, they would not have taken such a strong stand against the opposition. Why would anyone die for a lost cause or for a prefabrication?

The Scriptures tell us that God, in his sovereignty, raised Jesus from the dead through the power of the Holy Spirit—another cooperative work of the Trinity. As indicated earlier, Christ's death was no defeat. It was a victory over death that was confirmed on Resurrection Day. James Buswell says, "If Jesus only died, then death conquered him. But if Jesus died and rose again, then his death was a victory. When one believes in Jesus Christ as his personal Savior he, in effect, designates himself as representatively identified with Christ in his death and resurrection, and as living a renewed life by the power imparted to him by the risen Christ."[3]

Paul makes a strong statement when he says that Jesus "was declared with power to be the Son of God by his resurrection from the dead: Jesus Christ our Lord" (Romans 1:4). Thus his resurrection confirmed the word, the truth, and the ministry of Jesus. Because of his resurrection, we are able to call Jesus our Living Lord.

Just as Calvary is crucial for the existence of the Christian faith, so likewise is the resurrection. The Scripture says, "If Christ has not been raised, our preaching is useless and so is your faith" (1 Corinthians

15:14). In the same chapter we read, "And if Christ has not been raised, your faith is futile; you are still in your sins." This is categorical and definitive. God's plan of redemption would have failed. The resurrection was essential to the gospel. As Jesus said, "I am the resurrection and the life. He who believes in me will live, even though he dies" (John 11:25). Paul also emphasized that belief in the resurrection was necessary for salvation. He states, "That if you confess with your mouth, 'Jesus is Lord,' and believe in your heart that God raised him from the dead, you will be saved" (Romans 10:9).

If Jesus had not risen from the dead then we, as believers, have no hope for the future. Paul tells us that, "Christ has indeed been raised from the dead, the first-fruits of those who have fallen asleep" (1 Corinthians 15:20). The "first-fruits" mean that Jesus was the first to be raised from the dead with a gloriously changed body, which will be the identical resurrected body of all believers. Because of Christ's deity, death could not hold him and through that victory, believers are given the assurance of their own resurrection and life eternal.

HIS ASCENSION

Just as the resurrection completed the earthly mission of Jesus, so the ascension brought to a climax his ministry. We see such a logical sequence of events: the birth, the ministry, the death, the resurrection, and now the ascension of Jesus. As we consider the question of "Who is Jesus?" we recognize that all aspects of his life, either considered alone or collectively, point to his divinity.

The disciples watched as Jesus went skyward "on a cloud" or "in a cloud," which some have suggested may have been the cloud of God's glory. It is interesting that the angels talked about Jesus going into heaven, and we refer to the sky as "the heavens." Consequently, we imagine that heaven is upwards. If you remember the appearance of Jesus after his resurrection to the disciples when they were locked inside a room, he just appeared. With his newly resurrected body, Jesus was now moving in another dimension. He was no longer restricted to our time and space. Heaven is in a different dimension from ours. Yet it was necessary for the disciples, and for man, to see a visible ascension. Jesus could have easily just disappeared, but then there would have been no record of his departure. His physical ascension was a necessity.

Christ's ascension was also essential as a fulfillment of God's plan. Jesus explained to his disciples that it was necessary for him to go away because if he did not go away, "the Comforter would not come"— referring to the sending of the Holy Spirit. The Spirit was to empower them for their work of witness once Christ had returned to the Father.

The ascension moved Jesus from his earthly ministry into his ministry in the heavens. It was the link between the two. He moved from earth to be seated at the right hand of God the Father, where he intercedes on our behalf. We read, "Jesus, who went before us, has entered on our behalf. He has become a high priest for ever" (Hebrews 6:20). He became our Intercessor. He continues as our Mediator. He is our Advocate with God. He provides the mediation that we require and provides access into the very presence of God for every one of us. These are his priestly duties. He is Head of the Church and reigns over all.

Christ returned into the Father's presence where he was before he came to earth. In Jesus' priestly prayer before the cross, Jesus says, "And now, Father, glorify me in your presence with the glory I had with you before the world began" (John 17:5). Jesus was to return to his pre-existent state with the Father in the Godhead. The writer to the Hebrews talks about that return with these words: "After he had provided purification for sins, he sat down at the right hand of the Majesty in heaven" (Hebrews 1:3).

After donning servanthood and taking upon the likeness of man, Christ was returned by God to his rightful position. We read, "Therefore God exalted him to the highest place and gave him the name that is above every name, that at the name of Jesus every knee should bow, in heaven and on earth, and every tongue confess that Jesus Christ is Lord, to the glory of God the Father" (Philippians 2:9-11).

HIS SECOND COMING

When I was a teenager in the 1950s, not many Sundays could pass without hearing a sermon in our chapel on The Second Coming of Christ. The imminence of Christ's coming was preached with such fervency that one imagined the event would occur during the following week. In fact, it was so real to us that the sudden brightness in the sky from the sun emerging from behind the clouds was always a stark reminder of what had been preached on Sunday. Yet, here we are about sixty years later, and we are still waiting. Needless to say, we rightly hear from the pulpits today that it is still imminent. Time is not of the essence with God.

From a very rudimentary look at *eschatology*, which simply means the doctrine of the Last Things, one quickly ascertains that there are numerous interpretations and views on almost every aspect of the end times. Most of the personal understandings and interpretations relating to the future events differ in their chronological aspect. In other words, "when" these things are to take place and in what order they will occur is mostly what creates the divergent opinions.

There are differing views regarding whether the rapture (when the church is taken from this world) and the second coming of Christ are one and the same event. Some believe so, while others believe that they will be separated by a time of tribulation and the Second Coming will be when Christ returns with his saints for the battle of Armageddon and the beginning of his thousand year reign of peace. Some believe that the rapture will be secret, while others believe the opposite. Some believe that the rapture will be before the tribulation, some mid-tribulation, and others after the tribulation. So, dependent upon your understanding and belief, the rapture could occur at any moment while the second coming of Christ could be several years away because of events predicted in Scripture that are yet to take place. On the other hand, some teach that the signs of the times lend themselves already to an imminent return of our Lord.

In all of this discussion, there is no disagreement that Jesus will return. At the time of the ascension, the angels said to the disciples, "Men of Galilee, why do you stand here looking into the sky? This same Jesus, who has been taken from you into heaven, will come back in the same way you have seen him go into heaven" (Acts 1:11). Likewise, Jesus talked about this himself. On one occasion he said, "They will see the Son of Man coming on the clouds of the sky, with power and great glory" (Matthew 24:30). This was exactly how he ascended. Luke also records some of Jesus' words on the subject when he says, "For the Son of Man in his day will be like the lightning, which flashes and lights up the sky from one end to the other" (Luke 17:24). In discussing his departure with the disciples, Jesus comforts them with the words that he was going away to prepare a place for them. He then says, "And if I go and prepare a place for you, I will come back and take you to be with me that you also may be where I am" (John 14:3). Jesus promises he will return.

There are hundreds of references to the second coming of Christ in the Scriptures—over three hundred in the New Testament alone. It is not surprising that this topic should be prominent in our discussions. All through Jesus' ministry, he talked about events that were to come. He indicated that he would suffer at the hands of men, predicted that he would be put to death, assured the disciples that he would rise again on the third day—and all of these things occurred as he said. He told his disciples that he would be returning to the Father and then announced that he would come back. Why would anyone ever question the final prediction of his coming again, when all the others were duly fulfilled in his lifetime?

Jesus' emphasis in his teaching was for the church to be ready for his return. When asked when this would take place, his reply was that "It is not for you to know the times or dates the Father has set by his own authority" (Acts 1:7). He said that his return would be like a thief in the night when most would be unprepared for it. Life would be going on as normal with little thought about the cataclysmic world event to take place. For Christians, the prospect of the Second Coming should be a motivation for holy living. We should experience some excitement as we live anticipating and expecting his promised return.

Jesus died as the Suffering Servant but he will return as the Coming King. His power and his majesty will be overwhelming. The Scripture says that "every eye shall see him" (Revelation 1:7), which certainly does not imply it will occur in secret. For those who do not believe and have rejected Christ and the gospel, it will be a fearful time, but for believers it will be a time of rejoicing and celebration as we meet the Lord of Glory, the Lord we have loved and served.

WHO IS GOD THE SON?

Jesus is the second person of the Godhead, eternal, co-equal with God the Father and God the Holy Spirit. He was pre-existent within the Trinity before the foundation of the world. He humbled himself and took the role of servant, became flesh, identified himself with mankind, and freely offered himself as a supreme sacrifice so that man could receive forgiveness and salvation. During his earthly ministry, Jesus was fully God and fully man. He was the God-man, having both human and divine natures residing within him at the same time. As God was in Christ, we see in the Cross the self-substitution of God for our sin—an act of unconditional self-giving and love, both from the heart of God the Father and God the Son. This again is the God we serve.

QUESTIONS FOR GROUP STUDY

WHO IS GOD THE SON?

Reading: John 1:1–18

1. How is it that the world is ready to accept Jesus as "a good man" or a teacher or a prophet but finds it difficult to accept him as Savior and Lord?

2. Why is the deity of Jesus the critical and essential aspect of his being?

3. Why was the death of Jesus not a defeat? Could God have brought salvation some other way?

4. If there had been no resurrection, what would have happened to our faith, and why?

5. Why was it necessary that the disciples see Jesus ascend into heaven rather than Jesus just disappear?

6. Do you think the second coming of Jesus is emphasized enough in our churches today? Describe your feelings about the anticipated event.

5

WHO IS GOD THE HOLY SPIRIT?

"When he, the Spirit of truth, comes, he will guide you into all truth."
JOHN 16:13

I had been a Christian for twelve years before I came to a real understanding of God the Holy Spirit. Whether that was a sad commentary on me or those from whom I should have learned, I am not sure. It so happened that at that time I was working for **Christianity Today** and had the privilege of sharing the same office as Dr. Philip Hughes, the Anglican scholar. It was he who first pointed me to literature and information about the person and work of the Holy Spirit. He helped open my eyes to the operation and ministry of God's Spirit. I quickly came to understand, appreciate, and experience the reality of the Spirit's work and ministry.

For me, the Holy Spirit did exactly what was promised in the Scriptures. He gave me a fresh appreciation of the Word of God. He caused the person of Christ to be more real. He gave new spiritual vision, impetus, and motivation to my Christian walk.

That was at the time when the third person of the Trinity, the Holy Spirit, was not a popular subject from pulpits and—tragically—was too often misunderstood, maligned, or simply ignored. There was a certain vagueness among Christians as to who the Holy Spirit was and his role in the life of the believer. It seemed that people could handle the concept and existence of God the Father and God the Son, but the person and work of the Holy Spirit appeared somewhat difficult to grasp—thus, it was passed over. And because of this lack of understanding about the Holy Spirit, the whole subject was shrouded with much consternation and fear. Fortunately, that is not the case today.

HIS PERSONALITY

So we ask, "Who is God the Holy Spirit?" First and foremost, we must emphasize that the Holy Spirit is a person; he has a personality. An opinion poll taken several years ago suggested that many Christians still considered the Holy Spirit to be a symbol of the power of God without being a separate person within the Godhead. Many people refer to the Spirit of God as an "it" or an "influence" as opposed to recognizing that he is a person within the Godhead and shares co-equality with God the Father and with God the Son.

The Holy Spirit is intangible and invisible because he is spirit. As the third person of the Trinity, he enjoys the same attributes of omniscience, omnipresence, and omnipotence as God the Father and God the Son. He is also eternal and pre-existent. He is given many titles in Scripture: the Spirit of God, the Spirit of the Lord, the Spirit of Truth, the Spirit of Wisdom, Eternal Spirit, and others. He is considered the Source of life and the Giver of life. He is also represented in Scripture by the symbols of fire, water, and oil.

In the New Testament, we find that the actions of the Holy Spirit are those that pertain to a person. Jesus promised his disciples that once he had returned to the Father, the Holy Spirit would be sent to them and would come upon them. In doing so, he referred to him as a Comforter, a Counselor, and an Advocate, all names or titles that entail a state of being and doing. Jesus always referred to the Holy Spirit as "he." Referring to the coming of the Spirit, Jesus said, "But when he, the Spirit of truth comes, he will guide you into all truth. He will not speak on his own; he will speak only what he hears, and he will tell you what is yet to come" (John 16:13). Thus the Spirit can hear, speak, and guide. Jesus went on to say that the Spirit would teach, communicate, lead, convict, and testify to him, the Lord Jesus.

Paul advises believers to take care not to "grieve" the Spirit (Ephesians 4:30). We discover in the early days of the church that Peter asked Ananias, "How is it that Satan has so filled your heart that you have lied to the Holy Spirit?" (Acts 5:3). Only a person can be lied to or grieved. The Holy Spirit is very definitely a person, and we would do well not to allow appreciation of his work to overshadow his personality.

HIS PRESENCE IN THE SCRIPTURES

The Holy Spirit is mentioned in the Old Testament from the very first chapter of the very first book. In Genesis we discover that his activity commenced even before Creation. We read, "Now the earth was formless and empty, darkness was over the surface of the deep, and the Spirit of God was hovering over the waters" (Genesis 1:2). The Spirit of God was involved in the creation of the world. The Spirit's involvement in nature is also confirmed in the Book of Psalms. Referring in one place to earthly creatures, we read, "When you send your Spirit they are created, and you renew the face of the earth" (Psalm 104:30). Throughout the Old Testament books, we find constant references showing the activity of the Holy Spirit as it relates to special functions and special tasks.

Various people were given specific responsibilities and were empowered by the Spirit of God to carry out those responsibilities. For instance, we see Joseph was a recognized leader. Even Pharaoh asked the question, "Can we find anyone like this man, in whom is the spirit of God?" (Genesis 41:38). Joseph was given leadership qualities through the power and working of God's Spirit in his life. He was chosen to carry out the purpose and plan of God for his people in Egypt. It was similar for Moses. When life became too much for him in his attempt to lead the people, God said to him, "I will take of the Spirit that is on you and put the Spirit on them. They will help carry the burden" (Numbers 11:17). The Spirit of God was already resting upon Moses to fulfill his call in leading the people, but he needed help. Here we see God outlining his plan to bring his Spirit upon others to help Moses in the work.

The Scriptures clearly indicate that the Spirit of the Lord was upon Joshua, Gideon, and Samson, giving them supernatural abilities to fulfill their roles. Of Samson, we read, "The Spirit of the Lord came on him in power" (Judges 15:14). Saul and David were also anointed by the Spirit of God for the tasks they had to undertake. At the time of David's anointing as king, we read, "And from that day on the Spirit of the Lord came upon David in power" (1 Samuel 16:13). Likewise, Samuel, Elijah, and Elisha, the prophets of God, were filled with his Spirit to perform their ministry.

The Spirit was given not only for leadership or even spiritual ministry but also for skill and abilities. In speaking to Moses, God said, "I have chosen Bezalel…and I have filled him with the Spirit of God, with skill, ability and knowledge in all kinds of crafts—to make artistic designs for work in gold, silver and bronze" (Exodus 31:2-4). This was in preparation for making all the intricate and ornate trappings for inside the tabernacle.

We have already made reference to the Holy Spirit in the New Testament, particularly those passages that refer to his personality, but there is much more. He continues his special visits and anointing upon various people for specific reasons.

It was promised to Zechariah that his barren wife, Elizabeth, would have a child—but he would be no ordinary child. They would call him

John, a man chosen by God to announce the coming of the Messiah. The angel told Zechariah that his son would "be filled with the Holy Spirit even from birth" (Luke 1:15). This, of course, was John the Baptist, who ably fulfilled his role through the power of the Holy Spirit. Both his parents, Elizabeth and Zechariah, were also filled with the Holy Spirit (Luke 1:42 and Luke 1:67).

Probably the most well-known act of the Holy Spirit is, of course, his involvement in the virgin birth of Jesus. From her encounter with the angel Gabriel, Mary received the startling news that she would be with child prior to marrying Joseph, her betrothed husband. When she enquired, "How will this be?" she was told, "The Holy Spirit will come upon you, and the power of the Most High will overshadow you. So the holy one to be born will be called the Son of God" (Luke 1:35). This, of course, is exactly what happened. Mary gave birth to Jesus, conceived by the Holy Spirit. Thus we see the miraculous involvement of the Holy Spirit in the incarnation of Jesus. Here was the third person of the Trinity involved in the presenting of the Savior, the second person of the Trinity, to the world. The birth was supernatural in every sense.

If the work of God's Spirit could be measured in importance, the anointing of Jesus would rank very high. Jesus came to John the Baptist to be baptized. As he came out of the water, the Holy Spirit came upon him, anointing him with power for two reasons. Firstly, he was to be led into the desert for the next forty days, where he would suffer temptation; and secondly, it was at the commencement of his ministry. We are only told of three temptations he suffered over which he emerged victorious, and as the Scripture says, "Jesus returned to Galilee in the power of the Spirit" (Luke 4:14). From there he went into his three year ministry, operating in the power and with the enabling of the Holy Spirit. Jesus confirmed his anointing by the Holy Spirit when he referred to the prophecy from Isaiah, "The Spirit of the Sovereign Lord is on me, because the Lord has anointed me to preach the good news to the poor. He has sent me to bind up the brokenhearted, to proclaim freedom for the captives and release for the prisoners" (Isaiah 61:1). On beginning his ministry, Jesus went into the synagogue, read this portion of Scripture, and stated, "Today this Scripture is fulfilled in your hearing" (Luke 4:18).

HIS PRESENCE IN THE WORLD

Without the presence of the Holy Spirit, the world would be in an abysmal state. Whether we recognize it or not, the Holy Spirit works through the church and believers—who are the church—to bring an element of social conscience. Through this, the Spirit of God exercises a restraining influence upon our society. If he were not here, we would experience total anarchy.

It is true that we have law and order that present some semblance of deterrent, but look how quickly a peaceful protest turns into a riot. Even sports fans at times run amok, damage property, become violent towards others, and generally rebel against the authorities who represent the law. Without the Spirit of God in the world, this kind of activity would be even more prevalent.

As believers, we are temples of the Holy Spirit, and our lives testify to the presence of the Spirit. We form part of that restraining influence in a world bent on sin and rebellion, not just against human authority but against God. It is in that same arena that the Holy Spirit does his work upon the human heart.

The primary function of the Holy Spirit in the world is explained by Jesus when he said, "When he comes he will convict the world of guilt in regard to sin and righteousness and judgment: in regard to sin, because men do not believe in me; in regard to righteousness, because I am going to the Father, where you can see me no longer; and in regard to judgment, because the prince of this world now stands condemned" (John 16:8-11).

Jesus was explaining that after his crucifixion and ascension, the Holy Spirit's task would be to work upon the hearts of mankind.

What did Jesus mean? The sin of unbelief is rebellion and disobedience against God. The Holy Spirit's work is to bring men and women face to face with the reality of their sin: that unbelief is sin. He does this by convicting men of their sinful state as well as their false thinking and knowledge. In its place he presents the solution through Christ, the message of salvation. God's Spirit is called the Spirit of truth because he presents the truth of the gospel (John 14:17). He reveals Christ to the world. Through the suffering and death of Christ, true righteousness, God's righteousness, is revealed and is made available to those who believe. Against all odds, people are made righteous through Jesus Christ (Romans 3:22). He also declares the victory over the prince of this world, Satan, and announces that judgment has already been meted out, and this, for the benefit of all believers. All this is achieved through the ministry of the Holy Spirit.

The work of God's Spirit is integral in applying the gospel to mankind. If we do not understand who the Holy Spirit is, then it is difficult to comprehend the gospel. However, there are many people who enjoy the benefits of the gospel without fully understanding it, and likewise, many enjoy the benefits of God's Spirit without understanding him. The work of the Spirit in the world is to draw people to God, and he alone can carry out that mandate.

HIS PRESENCE IN THE CHURCH

The church would not, and could not, exist without the presence of the Holy Spirit. It is interesting that the ministry of Jesus was inaugurated by the anointing of the Spirit at his baptism, and the church was inaugurated by a collective anointing of the Spirit of God. The church was birthed at Pentecost. It was established when the outpouring of the Holy Spirit came upon the disciples, as Jesus promised. As they preached, over three thousand people came to faith in Christ on that day. That was the beginning of the Holy Spirit's work as the replacement or representative of Christ on earth. He ushered in the Age of the Spirit, in which we still live today.

Nearly one thousand years before Pentecost, the prophet Joel had foretold the coming of the Holy Spirit. Joel stated, "I will pour my Spirit on all people" (Joel 2:28). Peter preached to the people on the Day of Pentecost and indicated that they were seeing the fulfillment of that prophecy. Ezekiel also talked about a new day coming, when God spoke through him saying, "I will give you a new heart and put a new spirit in you; I will remove from you your heart of stone and give you a heart of flesh. And I will put my Spirit in you and move you to follow my decrees and be careful to keep my laws" (Ezekiel 36:26-27).

The Spirit of God was sent to empower the church, to be the life of the church; therefore, the church that ignores the Holy Spirit brings about its own spiritual downfall. No church can dishonor or grieve the Holy Spirit, either through ignorance or intentionally, and expect blessing upon its ministry. Its message to the world will be weak and insipid. The message of regeneration and reconciliation to God would be missing because it is only revealed and applied to man by the Holy Spirit. This kind of church is powerless and restricted to operate in the flesh. It is left with nothing but a charade of going through cold, lifeless motions—an empty liturgy. What a sad scenario! The church can never operate effectively without the working of God's Spirit.

The Holy Spirit came to be Christ's replacement upon earth. He continued on where the ministry of Jesus left off at the ascension. The church, a body of regenerate people worldwide, represents Christ to the world through the ministry of God's Spirit. The church is called the body of Christ, and Christ himself is the Head. It is also the temple of God's Spirit where his Spirit dwells through the lives of each believer, each one being considered "living stones" within that temple (1 Peter 2:5), and Christ being the "chief cornerstone" of that building. Paul tells us that "In him the whole building is joined together, and rises to become a holy temple in the Lord. And in him you too are being built together to become a dwelling in which God lives by his Spirit" (Ephesians 2:21-22). Individual believers are an integral part of the temple of the Lord. Christ's presence is known in the church, and through the church to the world, by the presence of the indwelling Spirit of God.

The Spirit upholds, strengthens, and supports the church in its spiritual function. He brings unity, love, and a oneness among its members. He enhances the worship, praise, and devotion within the hearts of the believers. He gives purpose, vision, and motivation to move forward as a body and to present Christ to the world. The gifts of the Holy Spirit are also given for the spiritual benefit of the church. It is true that they are conferred by the Spirit upon individual believers but are given to function within the church, enabling it to fulfill its calling.

There are a variety of gifts provided for those different functions (1 Corinthians 12:7-27). There are gifts of office, administration, of evangelism, of edification as well as other more supernatural gifts, but all for the sake of the collective body, not for the glory of any individual believer. Whatever gift we have been blessed with, we need to remember that, although we can preach, we cannot save, and although we can pray, we cannot heal. All activity that holds any eternal significance or spiritual achievement in the advancement of God's kingdom is totally orchestrated and conducted by the Holy Spirit. The purpose of the Spirit giving gifts is to enable the church to carry out its call to take the gospel to all men and to be the hands and feet of Jesus in expressing his compassion to a hurting and lost world.

HIS PRESENCE IN THE BELIEVER

Just as the Holy Spirit is essential to the world and the church, so his presence is imperative to the believer. Once a person becomes a Christian, the Spirit of God has already completed his work of regeneration, which is just another word for re-birth. Just as he was involved in Creation, so he is in the re-creation of man in his experience of becoming "born again." The real experience results in a true and genuine faith.

If we are Christians, then whether we know it or not, it was the Spirit of God who caused us to see ourselves as we were—people in need of salvation and reconciliation with God. It was he who brought us to faith in Christ and birthed us into the family of God. It is he who instigates the change in the heart and mind of man. No new Christian can be born without his involvement. Without him there would be no gospel and no Christian faith. But this is just the beginning of his work in the life of the believer.

Upon his return to the Father, Jesus promised that he and the Father would send the Holy Spirit to anoint and dwell within the disciples. As already mentioned, he called the Spirit the Comforter, the Counselor, the Advocate, and the Helper. It literally means "one who comes alongside," which was important for the disciples and for future believers. Since the time of Pentecost, when the Spirit came, all believers become indwelt by the Spirit of God at the point of conversion. Believers "are controlled not by the sinful nature, but by the Spirit, if the Spirit of God lives in you. And if anyone does not have the Spirit of Christ, he does not belong to Christ" (Romans 8:9). There is little to misunderstand in that reference. Christians become temples of the Holy Spirit, again as the Scriptures state, "Do you not know that your body is a temple of the Holy Spirit, who is in you, whom you have received from God?" (1 Corinthians 6:19).

It was the Holy Spirit who inspired the writing of God's Word, and it is he who goes on teaching and revealing the truth of that Word and the understanding of Scripture. He instructs the new believer in the truth of God as he guides us into all truth as Jesus promised he would. Just as we see in Luke's Gospel that the disciples were empowered for service by the Spirit of God, so he gives the Christian power to witness and to serve within the church.

For the believer, his very spiritual life is brought into existence by the Spirit of God. He gives new life in Christ and is the sustainer of that life. He provides strength and encouragement when needed on the Christian's spiritual journey. He pours God's love into our hearts that it might overflow to others (Romans 5:5), and that love produces unity in the church. The Spirit is also involved in the believer's prayer life as he grants access to the Father (Ephesians 2:18) and gives direction to prayer (Romans 8:26-27). He implements the will of God on earth through prayer.

However, in spite of what we have already seen, the primary task of God's Spirit within the believer is to enable him or her to become like Christ. Is that possible, you may ask? Yes, and No! As followers of Christ, we are called Christians, which means "Christ ones," indicating that we do attempt to imitate our Master. If we do that in our own strength, or as we say "in the flesh," then it is impossible. If, on the other hand, we allow the Holy Spirit to perform his ministry in us, then he provides the grace and strength for us to progress towards bearing the image of Christ. As believers, we are called to reflect the characteristics of Christ in our lives. Only as we allow the Spirit of God to take charge can that ever be achieved.

How can the life of the Spirit be expressed in our lives as believers? As the Holy Spirit indwells us, so the fruit of his presence should be reflected in our life. The fruit of the Spirit is love, joy, peace, patience, kindness, goodness, faithfulness, gentleness, and self-control (Galatians 5:22). These are also characteristics of Christ and, as such, can be and should be evident in our daily Christian walk. We shall discuss the fruit of the Spirit in greater detail further on in the book, but suffice it to say that this has to be the standard to which we should aspire. These are the essential qualities needed if we are to be image-bearers of Christ.

WHO IS GOD THE HOLY SPIRIT?

He is the third person of the Trinity, co-equal and co-existent within the Godhead. He it was who was involved in the creation of the world, in the incarnation of Jesus, the ministry of Jesus, and his resurrection. It was he who ushered in the Age of the Spirit and established the church of Jesus Christ and still applies the message of salvation to mankind. In fact, the regeneration of man—his spiritual rebirth—is the sole sovereign work of God the Holy Spirit. This too is the God we serve.

———————————————— ✕ ————————————————

QUESTIONS FOR GROUP STUDY:
WHO IS GOD THE HOLY SPIRIT?
Reading: John 16:5–16

1. What is your understanding regarding who the Holy Spirit is?

2. Do you think that there is some misunderstanding on the Holy Spirit within the church? Explain your answer.

3. What do you understand to be his work, both in the past and in the present?

4. How important is his work to the world and to the church?

5. What is the "Age of the Spirit," and why is it so called? What would the present age look like without the operation of God's grace and Spirit?

6. Are the gifts of the Spirit evident today within the church?

6

WHAT IS CHRISTIAN CONVERSION?

"If anyone is in Christ, he is a new creation."
2 Corinthians 5:17

England, that beautiful island bathed in history, was my birthplace. I discovered that long before my time, perhaps a century or two, it seemed that every rural village had its own parish church and its own small schoolhouse.

As decades passed, things changed. The young people went off to pursue higher education and never returned. Local farms became more mechanized, and fewer hands were required to tend the cattle and farm the land. Therefore, families left for larger towns and cities in search of employment. Gradually, the villages were bereft of people—and children in particular. For efficiency purposes, some of the schools had to amalgamate with other village schools. Consequently, there were village schools that stood empty and unused for many years.

Eventually, these schools became available for purchase, which allowed people to buy them and convert them into homes. Small, unused village chapels, as well as many old stone and wooden barns, also received the same treatment. With some ingenious renovations, those places were turned into beautiful homes. The process was simple.

A plan was drawn, the building was purchased, and the work crew came in and did the renovations. The building underwent a conversion.

The Christian's conversion is not dissimilar. God created the plan, Christ purchased the property (which was us), and the Holy Spirit implemented the plan in our lives through his work of regeneration. We needed to be reconstructed, to be made anew, to be re-birthed. That is a very succinct overview of the Christian conversion experience. However, the illustration of the renovation is not perfect, because whereas most conversions of physical properties are a work of renovation—a patching up of what is already there—this is not the case in Christian conversion. Christian conversion is a total makeover. A person experiences a total change followed by a completely new life. Let's take a closer look at that experience.

WHY DO WE NEED CONVERSION?

Every answer is preceded by a question, just as every solution is preceded by a problem. If Christian conversion is the solution, then we must ask, "What is the problem?" or "Why do we need Christian conversion?" If we are unable to recognize man's spiritual dilemma, then we will not see the need for spiritual conversion. The salvation of man is predicated upon his need to put right that which is wrong in his life. If we believe there is nothing wrong, then we will see no need for Christian conversion. God created man for himself, for communion and fellowship. God created man in his image. He created man in a perfect state, but man chose to exercise his freedom, and in his disobedience and rebellion against God, he brought upon himself a spiritual death sentence of incredible proportions. Subsequently, that sentence has been passed on to all generations, including those of us who are presently living.

Rebellion against God is sin. Nobody likes the word sin. Rarely is the gravity of sin acknowledged today. Sin is downplayed because it offends.

It has been minimized so that dishonesty, lying, and cheating are now accepted as normal in our society. We live in a culture of dishonesty. Deceit is the order of the day in business and in relationships. Lying is done openly without a second thought for its consequence. Immorality is reported without shame. Guilt has been eased. Wrongdoing seems only to be wrong if discovered.

However, all this is just a symptom of an underlying problem within the human heart. It does not take much intelligence to realize that there is a deep-seated problem in our society. I am not talking about the tragic and despicable events of years past, such as with Stalin and Hitler, but the violent and inordinate actions of man against man in the twenty-first century. We read in our newspapers of the sexual and physical abuse of women and children. We see unwarranted action by anarchists against authority and the Establishment. We see white-collar fraud and blue-collar theft. We see exploitation of the lower classes of society, manipulation of the system by those in authority, as well as corruption in governments around the world. All these are actions from the heart of men driven by hatred, greed, and self-centeredness. Although willing to agree that this is enough evidence of man's sinful nature, people are not so ready to admit it has anything to do with them personally.

Whether we like to acknowledge it or not, sin exists within all of us. We are inherently sinful. We did not have an option; we were born in sin. The Psalmist David said, "Surely I have been a sinner from birth, sinful from the time my mother conceived me" (Psalm 51:6). Do we ever have to teach our children to be disobedient, selfish, or greedy? Of course not. We find that we have to teach them just the opposite: to be obedient, courteous, and generous. How many times have we told our children to "be good"? The child's natural bent is to seek that which seems good for him or herself. Adults are also like that. Mature adult activity is little different from children except that the activity is of a different nature. Adults lie, cheat, steal, and kill to achieve their own ends.

As we look at individual mass murderers or some of the more recent dictators who have taken thousands of lives in their quest for power and control, we can only reiterate the words I recently heard a television commentator say: "How can ordinary people be so brutally evil?" The answer is that our natural bent is to sin, and although our personal intentions may be far from doing anything horrendous, the propensity to sin is always with us. This is the cause of the rift between us and God. While we deliberately remain in that state, we remain estranged from God and can have no relationship or reconciliation with him. But it is God who has provided the way for that rift to be abolished and the broken relationship to be healed.

The crux of this situation is that man is guilty before God for breaking his moral law, for blatant rebellion, and for disobedience. The outcome and penalty for our defiance is separation from God. As we have all sinned, we all have received this penalty. Yet it is God who has taken the initiative to lift the penalty from us. Man caused the problem, but God provided the answer. God could have ignored us and left us to "stew in our own juices," but he did not. Rather than abandon us, he provided the solution by giving his Son to die in our place.

We need forgiveness from God because it is against God that we have sinned. Forgiveness can only be received from the one we have wronged—and that is God. Sin originates in our pride and our arrogance as we go against God's authority. In fact, it could be said that deep down we have a desire to be God. Man is responsible for his sin—it is not simply a result of weakness or helplessness in controlling sin. It is a case of giving in to a natural disposition and succumbing to the sinful nature. We may try to excuse our sin, but there are no excuses. Although we are subject to outward influences, we cannot blame the environment in which we find ourselves, the peer pressure we might receive, our parents, or our upbringing. We are responsible and accountable for our own actions.

The bad news is that we are unable to correct the situation ourselves. Some try by "turning over a new leaf," but Christian conversion is nothing like that. There is nothing we can do to balance the scales. However, the good news is that it does not fall to our lot to do so. God has already done it. God did not have a duty or obligation to offer salvation but did so out of his love for mankind. God desires us to have a personal relationship with him and has supplied the means to bridge the gap, to bring about our reconciliation with him. He has provided salvation through the gospel of the Lord Jesus Christ, so let's look at the gospel.

WHAT IS THE GOSPEL?

The gospel is the central message of the Christian faith. This was the purpose of Christ's ministry and death. He was not just the messenger but the message. He came to bring life, and he was that life. Jesus said, "I am the Way, the Truth and the Life. No one comes to the Father except through me" (John 14:6). He came to bring the good news of salvation to mankind, so that man could experience the love of God, receive forgiveness of sin, and enter into a personal relationship with Jesus Christ. A relationship with Jesus is the purpose of the gospel. That relationship is distinctive, peculiar only to the Christian faith.

Forgiveness always has a price. My wife and I used to live in Eastern Canada, where ice storms were common in the winter. Shortly after one of those storms, I was out driving and turned the car down an on-ramp to join a freeway. Very quickly, I realized that the road was covered in ice as the car began to slide. I also noticed that there was a car turned sideways across the road at the bottom, totally blocking the entry to the highway. I attempted to steer my vehicle into the snow bank—to no avail. The brakes and the steering were useless. The lady in the car at the bottom sat helplessly awaiting the impact. I furiously scrambled for a way to lessen the damage, but, I too was helpless to avoid the collision.

Fortunately, my car had a very strong bumper, so I finished with a few scratches. Unfortunately, the same could not be said of the side panel of the other vehicle. I assumed that because I had run into her vehicle, the lady could have insisted that I was responsible. However, she indicated that obviously it was not deliberate or the result of carelessness, so she would take care of it herself. In essence, she forgave me, but she had to pay for the repairs.

There is always a cost to forgiveness, whether it is financial, physical, emotional, or mental. Think of two people in conflict. If there is to be forgiveness, then one person has to admit defeat or back down and swallow his pride. Either way, someone pays. It is the same with the forgiveness that man receives from God. God paid the price by giving his Son to die. Jesus paid the price for our forgiveness by giving his life on the cross. Why could not God, who is all-loving, just say, "I forgive you"? It is because it would not be true to his nature and character to do so. Let me explain.

God is holy and God is just. His holiness is such that God cannot entertain or look upon sin. We are kept from God's presence because of our sinful nature. Because he is just, he cannot let sin go unpunished. Because of his holiness, God cannot be indifferent to sin. Sin is repugnant to his nature and character, and all sin is against God. We dislike hearing or acknowledging God's wrath, but his wrath against sin is not an impetuous or sudden, uncontrolled outburst of anger. God's wrath is derived from his justice. His justice has to be satisfied, and as man is incapable of paying the price to satisfy that justice, God himself, out of his incredible love, stepped in and provided the solution. He is the judge who is forced to mete out the judgment but also the judge who steps down from the bench to personally pay the penalty as well.

Christ took the punishment for our sin on the cross. This is the heart of the gospel. No longer do we need to live under the sentence of death. No longer do we need to have a broken relationship with God.

By availing ourselves of this gift from God, we begin a new relationship with him and a new life in Christ.

When describing the gospel, it may seem as though I am reiterating that which has gone before in earlier chapters. This is inevitable, as all facets of the Christian faith find their foundation in the gospel. One cannot give due consideration to the workings of the gospel without referring back to the Trinity, because God gave his Son, the Son gave his life, and the Holy Spirit applies the gospel to mankind. We must also refer back to the nature and character of God. It is God's holiness and his abhorrence of sin, as well as his judgment against man's rebellion, that creates the necessity for the gospel. It is only by looking at the life and death of Jesus that we can see the expression of God's love in the giving of his Son to provide the gospel. The death of Jesus is central to the gospel, and the gospel is central to the Christian faith; therefore, it is essential that we understand the Cross and its implications. We are reminded by John Stott that, "God does not love us because Christ died for us. Christ died for us because God loved us."[1]

A simple sentence to outline the gospel is this: God is Holy, man is sinful, and the only way they can be brought together is through the plan instigated by God and carried out through the person and work of Jesus Christ. What it means bears some explanation. There are many Scriptures used for this purpose, the most common of which is this: "For God so loved the world that he gave his one and only Son, that whoever believes in him should not perish but have eternal life" (John 3:16). The next verse adds further explanation. "For God did not send his Son into the world to condemn the world, but to save the world through him" (John 3:17). Here we see the action of God the Father and his purpose in that action.

Paul explains to Timothy the reasoning and the heart of God in providing the gospel and the foundation upon which it is built. He says that God our Savior "wants all men to be saved and to come to a knowledge of the truth. For there is one God and one mediator between God and men, the man Christ Jesus, who gave himself as a ransom for all men" (1 Tim 2:4-6).

There are three facets outlined here that relate to the gospel. There is only one God, which we have already discussed. All others are the figment of man's imagination. It is important that we recognize who God is, his nature and character, his love, his holiness, and his justice, without which we can never understand our own sinfulness and need for salvation. We also see that it is God's desire that all men should avail themselves of this gift of salvation from him.

Conflict between two people or between employee and employer often requires the services of a mediator. The Scriptures indicate that once we recognize our need for salvation and our need to be reconciled to God, then we need a mediator to bring about that reconciliation. We cannot do it ourselves. That mediator is Christ Jesus. Through his life, death, and resurrection, God offers man the opportunity to be reconciled to Himself.

When a kidnapping takes place, it is usually followed by a ransom demand, the payment of which is supposed to earn the freedom of those kidnapped—often that is not how it ends in real life. The spiritual kidnapping I refer to here was of man's own choosing. He chose to go his own way and live a life captivated by sin and self. He rebelled against God who, by nature, had to mete out due punishment. The punishment was death, but Christ died as our substitute. Christ died for us while we were still in our sin. We read, "But God demonstrates his own love for us in this: While we were still sinners, Christ died for us" (Romans 5:8). His death made it possible for us to be pardoned, to be free from the penalty and punishment of sin. As John Stott so aptly puts it, "Divine love triumphed over divine wrath by divine sacrifice. The Cross was an act simultaneously of punishment and amnesty, severity and grace, justice and mercy."[2]

Jesus was the ransom payment to release mankind from the bondage of sin. Christ paid the price by giving his life so that man can have freedom from the captivity and dominion of sin and self. He was the perfect substitute because of his deity and because of his sinless life. He alone could die for the sins of the world because he alone was the perfect sacrifice to atone for man's sin. The Cross is the only basis for man's forgiveness.

This is the good news of the gospel, but how is it applied to the life of an individual?

WHAT HAPPENS AT CONVERSION?

Spiritual conversion of a person is often conceived long before conversion occurs. The heart and mind have been struggling with spiritual matters, usually for some time preceding this event. Some people ponder and consider all aspects of the Christian faith for years before making the final commitment. For others, it appears to be a spontaneous event that occurs with little pre-meditation. As unbelievers, there was nothing in us to cause us to make any move towards God—in fact, our sinful nature gave us the desire to move in the opposite direction—until the Holy Spirit began his work in us.

The work of God's Holy Spirit commences prior to any commitment to the faith. He does this by opening spiritual eyes. He creates an awareness of sin and the need for salvation. He reveals and gives us understanding of the gospel. Sometimes this process happens through adverse circumstances, like Paul—the stockbroker in our opening chapter who attended a friend's funeral. Sometimes God's Spirit uses other people to cross our paths, or he impresses us directly as we read from the Scriptures. After convincing us that things are wrong in our life and need to be put right, the Holy Spirit implants the faith so that a personal commitment can be made. He it is who draws the unbeliever to God, enabling the exercise of that faith in Christ and for regeneration to take place.

Regeneration, which means being made anew, is enacted completely by the Holy Spirit. What is it that we accept by faith? We accept that the death of Jesus is for us, that he died in our place and provides us the way to escape the penalty and punishment due for our rebellion against God. We turn away from sin in remorse and repentance, and appropriate the Cross of Christ by faith personally. Thus, we receive forgiveness of sin and are pardoned, and at that moment the Spirit of God comes to dwell within. This is the moment we become a child of God and are accepted into the family of God.

Salvation is totally from God's side. There is no contribution we could ever make towards our salvation. It begins and ends with the grace of God. If he punished us as we deserve, that would be justice. If he simply spared us the punishment, that would be mercy. Instead, he gives us salvation, which we do not deserve, and that is grace. We receive unearned and unmerited favor from God. Archbishop Hammond called this event a change from the "state of nature" to the "state of grace."[3]

This is the act of conversion. This is what is referred to as "being born again."

The term "born again" has become a term used both in and outside the church. It is sometimes used in secular settings when a person has seized an opportunity to recover from a life of failure and has successfully started over again. Mostly, however, it is used by evangelical Christians with reference to Christian conversion, although there are those within the church who do not like the term, because for them, it holds a concept of fanaticism. However, Jesus used the term, so we should be able to live with it. These were the words of Jesus, "I tell you the truth, unless a man is born again, he cannot see the kingdom of God" (John 3:3).

With the new Christian, there is a remarkable spiritual change—a spiritual rebirth. This change will not, and cannot, occur if the commitment was simply a mental or intellectual assent and nothing more. This is not just the adoption of a religious system or some nice new way of life. It is not just turning over a new leaf, like so many redundant New Year's resolutions. It is the commencement of a personal relationship with Jesus Christ. To become a true follower of Christ, there has to be a commitment from the heart as well as the head.

I have heard it said, "I believe all that you say, but I have never experienced anything as you have described." This is not uncommon. Stories are told of high-ranking clergymen and church leaders who have come to faith in Christ many years after serving within the church. Our status in society or in the church has no bearing on our acceptance or otherwise by God into the Christian faith. Either we have experienced new life and are in the family of God, or we are not. There are no half-measures. We might be good, do good, and even sit in a pew every Sunday morning, but all that is quite irrelevant when it comes to the gospel. Child or adult baptism does not replace true Christian conversion. We experience salvation only through the sacrifice of Christ.

If you are a true believer, then your new birth had a beginning. Whether or not you can pin it down to a date and time is not as important as being able to confirm that your faith in Christ now exists. Some ask whether the experience is gradual or instantaneous. The spiritual growth and the ensuing change in life are gradual, but the coming of the Spirit of God to dwell within a person must occur at a specific point in life, whether it was a conscious event or not. It is nonsense to say, "I have been a Christian all my life," because it is impossible for any one of us to be born a Christian. We had to be born again to become a child of God.

The gospel is mysterious for most of us because, to our natural mind, it does not make sense. It has no rationality. It is not logical. Why would

God do such a thing—to mete out the punishment and then pay the penalty? I have a friend who is a retired teacher. He told me that he was teaching a class of Asian and Indian students. He asked them if they understood the meaning of Christmas and Easter. Needless to say, they only knew them as holidays or mythical celebrations of some kind. When my friend explained the real meaning of Christmas and Easter, at their request, one student replied, "I have never heard such a ridiculous idea in all my life." Most other students took the same view. This confirms the Scripture when it says that the message of the Cross is foolishness to those who do not believe but that "God was pleased through the foolishness of what was preached to save those who believe" (1 Corinthians 1:21).

Understanding the gospel is not just an intellectual exercise of comprehension; it calls for a spiritual awareness that comes to us by the Holy Spirit. We read, "The man without the Spirit does not accept the things that come from the Spirit of God, for they are foolishness to him, and he cannot understand them, because they are spiritually discerned" (1 Corinthians 2:14). That is a quite a definitive statement and makes sense of the student's response.

Some consider that making a commitment to the Christian faith is taking a leap of faith into the dark. That idea is nullified when we realize that God the Holy Spirit has opened the heart and the mind to spiritual things. He called us to himself as we discover in Paul's letter to the church at Thessalonica where we read, "because from the beginning God chose you to be saved through the sanctifying work of the Spirit and through belief in the truth. He called you to this through our gospel" (2 Thessalonians 2:13). Once we were confronted with our sin, which was the problem, and then shown the solution—the forgiveness and salvation through Jesus Christ—the commitment was made from an informed position. I repeat, without the work of God's Spirit, the gospel will never be effective or applied. However, once applied to our lives, what is the result?

WHAT'S THE RESULT OF CONVERSION?

Christianity is not "pie in the sky when we die," as some like to indicate. It's certainly not pie and it's not in the sky, and we don't have to wait until we die. So the saying is wrong in every way. Certainly, there are eternal rewards for the Christian that come after life, but the enjoyment of his faith begins here and now in the immediate. Conversion has happened. Rebirth has taken place. New life has begun. So what now? Where does this leave the believer?

Because a deeply spiritual event has occurred, it will result in a noticeable change. For some it is dramatic and instantaneous, while for others the evidence of what has happened is a gradual process but very real, nonetheless. What has taken place is that the whole person has been transformed. Referring to this transformation in a person's life, the Scripture says, "he is a new creation; the old has gone, the new has come! All this is from God who reconciled us to himself through Christ" (2 Corinthians 5:17-18)—thus the change! Everything becomes as new. Some people have said that everything—nature, people, the world, and life itself—appears to take on a new freshness. Why is this? It is simply because the person has become a new being. The heart and the mind have been changed, and life is viewed from a new perspective.

Through conversion, we are made right with God. The broken relationship we had with God is now repaired. We are now reconciled to God. We received forgiveness and are pardoned from the sentence brought upon us by sin. That penalty has been removed, and we have no more condemnation over our heads. In Romans we read, "Therefore, there is now no condemnation for those who are in Christ Jesus" (Romans 8:1). The term "in Christ Jesus" is a scriptural term for those who, through conversion, have become children of God. As his children, we can now enjoy fellowship and communion with God as our Father.

Many times the Scripture refers to the believer as being "in Christ." Paul says, "It is because of him (God) that you are in Christ Jesus" (1 Corinthians 1:30). Christ lived a perfect life and died as a sinless sacrifice to atone for man's sin. When man responds to God's call of salvation, then his sin is attributed, or imputed, to Christ while Christ's righteousness, or perfection, is attributed, or imputed, to man. In other words, our sin is transferred to him, and his righteousness is transferred to us. The explanation from Scripture reads, "God made him who had no sin to be sin for us, so that in him we might become the righteousness of God" (2 Corinthians 5:21). Once this has happened, God sees us through Christ and declares us righteous. Thus, we are now "in Christ." Christ lives in us through the indwelling Holy Spirit, and we live in Christ through the faith we exercised in the sacrifice and death of Christ. However, although we are "in Christ," we are not sinless, and we do not lead perfect lives, but more about that is coming in our next chapter.

Our new position is a position of privilege. We read, "Therefore, since we have been justified through faith, we have peace with God through our Lord Jesus Christ" (Romans 5:1). Being justified simply means we have been made right with God; the relationship with him is back to what he intended in the first place. Talking about God the Father's sacrifice of his Son, the Scriptures say, "he did it to demonstrate his justice at the present time, so as to be just and the one who justifies the man who has faith in Jesus" (Romans 3:26). God is the One who justifies us, and now we are at peace with him. Being justified has been likened to a criminal awaiting his sentence who receives total pardon and at the same time is accepted as a new member of a wealthy family. This is the picture of us being forgiven and accepted into the family of God.

But all this is just the beginning. We now have a life of growing spiritually. This process is called sanctification. Sanctified means we are set apart by God, for God. The sanctification process is a lifelong development of our relationship and our walk with God. We learn what he wants for us, and from us, so that we seek to become the person he wants us to be. Our relationship with God is of primary importance. As we grow spiritually, we develop a deeper relationship. Just as normal relationships grow deeper and closer, so also grows our relationship with God.

There is no greater evidence of the effectiveness of the gospel than a changed life. In the past, we have known a New York gang member who became a New York evangelist. We have known a "Hell's Angel" biker who became an ordained pastor. I know a man who was once a very successful whiskey salesman; today he is a pastor. Perhaps these may seem extreme illustrations, but they do confirm the veracity and the power of the gospel. Such radical and long-lasting changes are difficult for skeptics to challenge. The Scripture plainly teaches that the gospel is for all and has the power to change lives. Paul says, "I am not ashamed of the gospel, because it is the power of God for the salvation of everyone who believes" (Romans 1:16). There is no level of society, either high or low, to which the gospel cannot reach and change lives. For most of us, the gospel has come to us in our ordinary lives by the faithful sharing and teaching of parents, and church leaders.

Books by Malcolm Gladwell, such as *The Tipping Point* and *The Outliers*, tell us that scientific research has shown that we are what we are because of our geography of birth, the nationality of our parents, and the environment in which we have been raised. Although there is an element of truth in this, some people like to suggest that what we believe is also derived from the same phenomena. If this is true, then we would expect more uniformity in geographical belief systems, but this is not the case. There are people in the West who have converted to eastern religions, while there are people in the East who have converted to Christianity. Then there are those whose parents have conscientiously taught their children the beliefs of Christianity only to see their children walk away from those beliefs. There are also many people who have had no Christian background but who have wholeheartedly embraced Christianity with enthusiasm. The evidence shows faith is a personal choice determined by the understanding of the truth.

Coming to faith in Christ, we discover that we must appropriate the gospel for ourselves. It must be a personal faith in Jesus Christ and not simply following the convictions of our parents. I know one lady who had been in the church for many years and had practiced the teaching of her parents because she thought that was the right thing to do, and yet she made this statement to friends: *It was not until I took the Alpha course that I came to a personal faith in Jesus Christ.* It was when she came to be presented with the truth of the gospel that she realized there was no reality to her Christian faith.

Our faith cannot be secondhand. It cannot be based upon another's faith, be they parents, teachers, or elders. We cannot work for it. We cannot earn it. It is not achieved by doing what the church or denomination expects of us. Salvation is ours totally by the grace of God. It is revealed through the Word of God and through the work and ministry of the Holy Spirit in our lives. This new relationship we have is confirmed by the Holy Spirit for "the Spirit himself testifies with our spirit that we are God's children" (Romans 8:16).

Having come to faith in Christ and having experienced Christian conversion, what now? Where do we go from here? We all have ideas of what might be expected of us once we formally call ourselves Christian, and while there are expectations, they are not usually as formidable as one might imagine.

The Christian life is a life full of purpose and meaning. It is not until we begin to comprehend the privileged position of being in the family of God and the vast blessings of being a child of God that we get a glimpse of the magnificence of this new life in Christ. Not only do we experience a previously unknown joy, but we have an incredible peace and a sense of security as we learn that God, in his sovereignty, is in control of everything. We respond to God our Father with gratitude and thanksgiving. We offer him our devotion, and our worship of him becomes real. We constantly remind ourselves that we did not find God; it was God who found us.

We discover an eagerness to learn and grow. Some people devour the Scriptures and spend much time in prayer. As we develop in our discipleship and as we grow in our Christian faith and walk, we recognize the process will not happen overnight. Often we are excited about what we discover and want to share with others the truth we find. Our lives become a series of glorious victories and disappointments. However, when we fall, with God's help we pick ourselves up, learn, and move on in the strength he gives. With this in mind, it presents us with the question that, if God is now in control of our lives, why do things not always work out smoothly in our Christian life?

QUESTIONS FOR GROUP STUDY:
WHAT IS CHRISTIAN CONVERSION?
Reading: John 3:1-21

1. Why is Christian conversion necessary?

2. Who is involved in a person's conversion experience? Who creates the initiative for a person to consider the Christian faith?

3. What does one do to become a Christian?

4. What actually takes place at the point of conversion?

5. What does it mean that conversion is by grace and faith alone?

6. Is it possible for a person to be converted and show no evidence of change in his or her life? Explain your reasoning.

7

WHY IS BEING A CHRISTIAN SO DIFFICULT?

"For our struggle is not against flesh and blood."
Ephesians 6:12

Under communism, Romania was a harsh country for Christians. They were harassed, constantly arrested and interrogated, persecuted, and imprisoned. Some died because of such experiences. My wife and I had a young man in his thirties stay with us who had suffered unjustly at the hands of the Romanian authorities. His name was Constantin, an ordinary man with a job and a family who was keen to help his pastor—especially in the distribution of Bibles. Early one evening, he borrowed his pastor's car to deliver some Bibles. Unfortunately, he was stopped by the police, and the Bibles were discovered.

Immediately, he was told to get out of the car and was arrested for what he thought was "possession of Bibles." But that was not the charge. As he opened the door, it inadvertently swung out and hit one of the policemen, resulting in a scratch on the back of the man's hand. For that, Constantin was charged with premeditated murder of a police officer. He was sentenced to seven and a half years in prison.

His prison experience was horrific. His treatment was brutal. The dormitory held fifty men with one toilet and two small wash basins. There was a constant line to use these facilities. They slept on iron beds, were given blankets full of bed bugs, and the lights were never turned off. The food was vile, but the prisoners were so hungry they would eat anything, including the worms or maggots in the rotting food. Breakfast came at 5:15 a.m. and consisted of one slice of bread and tea. Then, for lunch, they were given a small serving of corn mush (boiled maize) and a small helping of soup. This was served at 2:30 p.m. The evening meal arrived at 9:00 p.m. and usually consisted of a few spoonfuls of boiled wheat or vegetables.

The cells were so secure that guards had to unlock three doors to get in, yet the prison regimen was to count the prisoners twice a day: once at 7:00 a.m. and again at 7:00 p.m. At those times, the prisoners were forced to stand with their faces just a few inches away from the wall; they would have to stay in that position for up to two hours.

To say that prison life was harsh is a gross understatement. The threat of physical punishment, including torture, was never far away. The dormitories were rife with informers, people who would report on other prisoners to earn an early release. It was virtually impossible to communicate with others for fear of an informant overhearing. One word spoken against the authorities—or to question your sentence— meant certain punishment, the worst of which was solitary confinement. You were made to stand up without a break from 5:00 a.m. until 10:00 p.m. on the cold cement floor in complete darkness. The floor was the toilet, and food was served every other day.

Constantin said that a boy in the same dormitory, due to be released within a few days, became so weak that he could not get out of bed. The guards beat him until he was unconscious and then threw him onto the floor of a "solitary" cell. The next morning, he was found dead. Such was the cruelty in the prisons of Romania. Constantin himself was beaten with the leg of a table and other physical tortures about which he could not share with anyone, not even his wife.

The Church in the West heard about the plight of Constantin and the injustice of his situation. Prayer vigils were organized and a writing campaign was instigated from both the United Kingdom and the United States. It was estimated that more than 5,000 letters were sent to the Romanian embassies of these two countries. This action surprised the Romanian authorities. Constantin's sentence was reviewed and, ultimately, he was released. He had served one year in prison. He and his family were deported to the West, which was how he came to be visiting us. The family eventually settled in the United States.[1]

Constantin suffered because he was a Christian and for no other reason. Although even today there is persecution against believers around the world, and literally thousands are being imprisoned, tortured, or murdered, that is not the form of opposition discussed in this chapter. It is true that we have opposition from outside, quite minor in comparison, but we do have very real opposition from the inside. We need to look at both; but first, we need to ask a question.

IS YOUR FAITH REAL?

If your faith is not real, then why would you ever receive opposition? Satan is not concerned with people masquerading as believers—they are no threat to his kingdom. For our faith to be real, we must have experienced the new birth. We must have a personal relationship with Jesus Christ. There is no reason for a non-existent faith ever to be challenged—but authentic faith will be.

There is a vast difference between being religious and embracing Christianity. Even communism is a religion. Probably the greatest hindrance to true Christianity is religion. Religion with its bells and whistles, its liturgy and icons, tends to move the focus and attention away from God and turn it towards the performance of the rites. This fulfills a mental obligation of meeting the required worship of the Almighty but achieves nothing regarding the personal relationship between God and the worshipper.

Many people embrace a religion of convenience, but this is not Christian faith.

John Rock, one of the inventors of the birth control pill was, ironically, a staunch Roman Catholic. He was rarely absent from the 7 a.m. mass in his local church. Yet when the declaration was made from Rome in 1968 that all artificial methods of contraception were against the teachings of the Catholic church, John Rock's faith faded. When interviewed a year before he died, he was asked whether he believed in the afterlife. "Of course I don't," he replied. He went on to say "Heaven and Hell, Rome and all the church stuff—that's for the solace of the multitude. I was an ardent practicing Catholic for a long time, and I really believed it all then." [2] One wonders what his faith was based upon. This is not dissimilar to what I read in an autobiography of a well-known writer who said, "I believe in God but I have no time for organized religion," by which he implied he had a faith but chose to ignore the church. He considered the church unnecessary.

Unfortunately, in all branches of the church there are those who go through the religious motions, fulfill all the expected activities, but show no evidence of changed lives. Recently, the church has used extreme measures to encourage outsiders to enter its doors, and for many people that has turned out to be the most wonderful thing that has ever happened to them. However, there has been a downside. In making the church more accommodating and accepting, some have watered down the message to make it more palatable. In other words, the gospel has been compromised.

There is nothing wrong with being seeker-sensitive or acting in a way that is seeker friendly. It is wrong, however, when the focus shifts so that the methodology becomes the end in itself and moves the attention away from the message. Even Paul was willing to "become all things to all men" so that he might win some, but his message remained strong, unchanged, and undiluted, because there is only one gospel. In its enthusiasm to reach out, the modern church can be found guilty of offering a one-sided message. That message simply becomes "God loves you," which is true, but it becomes meaningless when it is not seen in the context of the entire gospel.

Why would we ever water down the gospel for the sake of it being accepted when we know that only those whose minds and hearts have been prepared by the Spirit of God will accept the gospel? Our responsibility is to faithfully share the whole gospel and nothing less. Also, when we concentrate just on the recipient of the gospel, we are in danger of becoming unfocussed upon Christ, who brought salvation, and the Holy Spirit, who instigates and provides the work of regeneration.

When Jesus talked to Nicodemus, he did nothing to soften the message. It was "I tell you the truth, unless a man is born again, he cannot see the Kingdom of God" (John 3:3). On another occasion, Jesus talked with the rich young ruler and did nothing to stop him walking away, even though he had heard how much the young man lived according to the law. The truth is the truth, which is accepted or rejected. No manipulation or coercion from us is right or necessary. We cannot force anyone to accept the Christian message. Therefore, there is no need for us to minimize the cost of becoming a follower of Jesus.

We ask the question, "For whose benefit is the gospel and for whose benefit is salvation?" One immediately imagines the recipient would be the answer, but just as God made mankind for himself, he provided salvation so that both could enjoy fellowship together. So whereas we are the beneficiaries of the gospel, it is fulfilling God's desire for us to have a personal relationship with him.

As real followers of Christ, our faith is based upon the unexpurgated gospel, and life becomes undeniably different. This is inevitable. One cannot have an encounter with God and not be changed. Every aspect of life becomes different. If life does not change, then a genuine conversion is in question. We acquire a different set of values, a different viewpoint, a different outlook on the world, and a different purpose in life. The path has changed. The objectives have changed. Because this act of regeneration has turned our faces God-ward, our thoughts, opinions, and desires have also changed. We become spiritually affected as well as intellectually, emotionally, and morally affected. In fact, the whole course of life takes on a different direction. However, going down that road is not without its obstacles; hence we come to the question, "Why is living the Christian life so difficult?

The simple answer is that we are at war. Paul indicates that "our struggle is not against flesh and blood, but against the rulers, against the authorities, against the powers of this dark world and against spiritual forces of evil in the heavenly realm" (Ephesians 6: 12). These spiritual forces war against the truth, and as individual believers holding the truth, we are susceptible to such opposition. But that warfare is twofold. Firstly, within our selves there is a war against sin; and secondly, there is an external spiritual war against the body of Christ, the church of Jesus Christ, of which we are part. Thus we feel the effects of that opposition.

THE WAR WITHIN

The war which exists within the Christian is a war between two natures, the old sinful nature and the new, spiritually alive nature in Jesus, evidenced by the indwelling Holy Spirit. The believer stands, sometimes pulled one way and then the other way. The apostle Paul confesses his struggle in this area, and we can identify with him. Understanding his spiritual experience, his faithful work for the kingdom of God, and the incredible letters he wrote to the early churches, we find it difficult to even imagine that Paul struggled with right and wrong. Yet he states clearly that "When I want to do good, evil is right there with me"

(Romans 7:21). He went on to say that the things he wants to do, he does not do and the things he does not want to do, he finds himself doing. We might think, "What chance is there for me if that was Paul's situation?" Well, we can be encouraged to find that he never threw in the towel, in spite of his declared struggle. Even if we struggle as Paul did, we too are blessed to have the same resources that he had to enjoy victory over the sinful nature.

Paul talks much about the struggle between the old nature and the new. He talks about sin being a deceiver waiting to lead him astray. He describes the internal conflict and the attempt of the sinful nature to control and master him. The awareness of sin was ever present with him. His intentions were good; he wanted to do right, but the inclination to do wrong was always there. The believer's experience today is no different. We all experience the struggle.

Although Paul blamed sin for his undesired actions, he was not avoiding responsibility but simply explaining the conflict. He admits that "I know that nothing good lives in me, that is, in my sinful nature" (Romans 7:18). Sin resides within the heart of every person. Sometimes we may consider it inactive, but it just awaits opportunity. Once aroused, sin can wreak havoc, particularly within the life of a Christian. Sin expresses itself through the mind and ultimately through the body. James says that desire gives birth to sin, and sin, when fully matured, gives birth to death (James 1:15).

Can we sin? Yes, we can! Are we immune to sin? No! Do we want to sin? Not if we are living for Christ. But we do sin, whether or not we like to admit it. Even if we do not succumb to immorality, the sin of jealousy, selfishness, pride, and other sins of the mind are never far away. As human beings, we are tempted to be dishonest and to do things that are to our advantage, even if a little questionable. We might even think that no one will know and it's not hurting anyone—neither of which is correct. God always knows, and you are usually hurting yourself. We live with the propensity to sin. We are no better or different from others when it comes to temptation.

However, real Christians have no excuse for habitually sinning. John talks about this in his epistle and declares that believers do not go on sinning. He is referring to the deliberate act of sin, not the slip-up or the disappointment or the unintended act. He indicates that the desire of the believer has changed, and no longer should sin hold the same attraction. Sinning should not be automatic, as it once was in our lives, because sin should no longer be the master—unless we allow it! However, there is no sinless perfection for the believer, however much we would like to ascribe to that belief.

But what has happened? There is now a vast difference between how we were, which is described in the book of Ephesians as "gratifying the cravings of our sinful nature and following its desires and thoughts" (Ephesians 2:3), to our becoming followers of Christ and enjoying victory over sin because of the indwelling power of the Holy Spirit. Becoming a new creation in Christ brings with it the strength and the power to overcome the previous bondage to sin. Yet along with it comes the comfort that even when we do fall and succumb to sin, we have an advocate, the Lord Jesus Christ, who intercedes with the Father on our behalf. An advocate is like a lawyer who intervenes for us, so aptly described by John when he states, "I write this to you so that you will not sin. But if anybody does sin, we have one who speaks to the Father in our defense—Jesus Christ, the Righteous One" (1 John 2:1). That forgiveness, however, is no excuse for sinning.

To fully understand the forgiveness that is so readily ours, we need to understand grace. We touched on this in the last chapter when we talked about receiving salvation and the fact that it was totally from God's side. We saw that grace was not just something which we received freely—which it is—but in receiving grace, we are given something absolutely opposite to that which we deserved. The act of God's grace is beyond human reasoning. Being pardoned and constantly forgiven by God when we deserve to be punished is difficult to comprehend. In fact, one reaction to the concept of biblical grace is, "If we can never sin beyond the reach of grace, why should we concern ourselves about sinning?"

Paul faced similar faulty reasoning when he rhetorically asks, "Shall we go on sinning so that grace may increase?" His answer was: "By no means! We died to sin; how can we live in it any longer?" (Romans 6:1-2). If we have died to sin, it really is no longer our master. As Paul says, "For sin shall not be your master" (Romans 6:14). Sin no longer holds dominion over us. Salvation releases us from that imprisonment. We enjoy a new freedom. But Paul warns about misusing the freedom given to us when he writes to the church at Galatia. He says, "You, my brothers, were called to be free. But do not use your freedom to indulge the sinful nature" (Galatians 5:13), highlighting the need for spiritual discipline in the exercise of that freedom in Christ. We have the freedom to say "No" to sin. It was the death of Christ that broke the power of sin so that the believer can experience victory over temptation and win the battle in the struggle between the old and the new nature.

It would be nice if, once we made the decision to follow Christ, we matured overnight in spiritual matters and that everything fitted into place. Unfortunately, that is not how it works in practice. In the new Christian walk, the warfare begins at day one and continues for a lifetime. Initially, we bring baggage into the Christian faith from our previous life and living. We have ideas, concepts, and philosophies that manifest themselves in our habits. Usually these habits do not disappear overnight, although it is possible for that to occur. For some people the changes are instantaneous whereas, for others, it takes time to rid themselves of inappropriate behavior. Paul recognizes this when he encourages new believers to make proper choices and take deliberate steps to spiritual maturity, to "put off the old" and to "put on the new."

We find that these steps come about as we experience the ministry of the Holy Spirit in our lives.

The good news is that, as we make those choices with the help of God's Spirit, sin begins losing its control over us. As the Scriptures indicate, sin is no longer our master. Jesus settled that issue at the cross. Paul shows how it affects the believer when he says, "our old self was crucified with him so that the body of sin might be rendered powerless, that we should no longer be slaves to sin" (Romans 6:6). We are exhorted to "not let sin reign in your mortal bodies" (Romans 6:12). There is a gradual release from the power and dominion of sin, although sin will never be totally eradicated. The fallen nature will always be present.

We cannot attain sinless perfection, as we have mentioned previously, but as we grow spiritually and our walk with God becomes closer, so the desire for sinful ways and habits diminish. As we grow in grace and in our understanding of Scripture, spiritual maturity gives us greater control over temptation and sin. A major antidote to sin is meditation, prayer, and praise. It is difficult to sin or to be tempted to sin when in communication with our Father or meditating upon Scripture. Likewise, while we live in an attitude of gratefulness and praise, it lessens the onslaught of temptation. When Jesus was tempted, he rebutted Satan with quotations from Scripture. Each time he was tempted, Jesus came back with the words, "It is written" (Matthew 4:4-10). If the Lord did this, we can do no better than follow his example! To do so requires our meditation and study of the Scriptures so that the Spirit of God can bring them back to mind when needed.

While we walk through the battle-zone of sin, it is good to remember that we cannot lose our salvation if we commit sin. If we could, then our salvation would be dependent upon our behavior, which is, of course, not biblical. If we believe that our salvation is affected by our behavior, then we nullify the work of Christ on the cross. We cannot be saved by our works. As the Scriptures teach, we are saved through grace by faith (Ephesians 2:8).

THE WAR WITHOUT

On a visit to Alaska, my wife and I had the pleasant experience of seeing salmon swimming upstream to their spawning grounds. That remains one of nature's spectacular events, to see that salmon—at the end of their lives—can exhibit such enormous strength to swim against such a current, even jumping rapids and rocks to get where they know they need to go. The Christian life is not dissimilar. Our society is definitely non-Christian, if not anti-Christian, so that a real Christian faith will always experience swimming against the current.

As Christians swimming against the tide, we have to combat the obstacles that seek to destroy us spiritually. But should we expect anything less? Jesus promised that "In the world you will have trouble" (John 16:33). He also said, "If they persecuted me, they will persecute you also" (John 15:20). Why then should we be surprised when we run into the head winds of opposition? We should be surprised if it is absent.

If a Christian dares to go against society because of his interpretation of Scripture, he is considered a bigot. If Christians take a stand against certain social issues, they are accused of being intolerant and politically incorrect. Consequently, it is openly suggested that Christians should change their thinking and adapt to present-day society. But truth does not change, nor can it, simply to fit the constant changes to the standards of society.

Society adopts new standards supposedly backed by the majority of the population. Yet the population has not necessarily demanded them but silently appears to be accepting of them. Thus, the opinions and standards of the minority become subservient to the rule of the majority, Christian or non-Christian.

For hundreds of years, Christians have historically held their principles that are based firmly upon Scripture, while man's "new wisdom" creates a changed society based upon the whims, wishes, and opinions of those in power. Therefore, Christians are expected to conform to the secular world's thinking, which is totally opposed to Paul's teaching to "not be conformed to the pattern of this world" (Romans 12:2). Thus it becomes difficult for the Christian to take his stand in the world without appearing to be closed-minded and unaccepting. Christians face this confrontation at schools, at work, mixing with society in general, and even within the home.

During my childhood, our family attended a small church in the east of England, the denomination of which was called "The Peculiar People." Everyone thought it a strange name but, in fact, the denomination had taken its name directly from Scripture where the Authorized Version states, "You are a chosen people, a holy nation, a peculiar people" (1 Peter 2:9), indicating not strange or weird, but a people set apart, belonging to God, peculiar to God. The scriptural title went along with being chosen as a people of God, but those outside the church would have no idea of this concept. Consequently, it was not easy for us young people to face our peers in school. We were thought of as "peculiar." Even some of the school teachers made the odd derogatory remark.

However, being publicly ridiculed over a name is miniscule opposition compared to that of being imprisoned and killed for one's faith. But even in seemingly minor situations of opposition, we must be willing to stand up and be counted. We used to be told from the pulpit to "pin your colors to the mast," which comes from flying the flag of the country you represent. We represent a kingdom not of this world, and we should be unashamed to fly the flag.

Living in the West, we enjoy what society calls "our rights" (although these may be subtly diminishing for the Christian now). We find it difficult to comprehend that in other countries Christian young people are devoid of rights to attend further education like college or university. Being denied higher education forces them to take more menial work with no prospect of advancement. Before the collapse of communism in Russia and Eastern Europe, many Christians were forced from positions of leadership and teaching, leaving them to improvise and trust God to provide for their families. How would we react to such an edict if it came upon us in the West?

Being a Christian in an anti-Christian society inevitably brings opposition. If you work in a secular setting, you will know that sometimes the opposition is blatantly obvious and at other times subtle. We find ourselves subjected to facetious and sarcastic remarks, to open isolation or refusal to communicate, even when our actions have not called for such treatment. Why is this?

It arises from the fact that the Christian is different. Our concept and philosophy of life is different. Our actions are governed by different principles, making our behavior stand out. Consequently, the presence of a real Christian will often bring a sense of guilt and condemnation to a non-Christian. The Christian represents the existence of God, which can be disturbing because some do not wish to acknowledge God's existence. It brings accountability, and that is unwelcome. Striking out at the Christian seems the best way to defend oneself against the truth he represents. Others have had a negative experience with the church or other Christians and have become skeptical of the Christian faith. Generally, these people have never experienced real Christianity, but their experience resulted in cynicism and criticism. Nonetheless, the Christian receives opposition as a result and again, although it is not persecution, it proves to be uncomfortable in the work place.

We all want to have that sense of belonging and want to be accepted by our colleagues, but we can feel that our Christian faith stands in the way. Opposition can cause us to keep quiet, to retreat, and to play down our Christian commitment for the sake of other people's feelings and views. This is sad but true. We want to be gracious and exercise tolerance, but at the same time we want to be open about our Christian faith and the reality of the gospel in our lives. Do we keep a low profile, or do we disturb the comfort zone of the non-believer? I believe we are called to be ourselves, to be true to our faith, but to exercise love and understanding towards those who do not believe or who do not want to believe.

Many years ago I was interviewed for a job as a currency trader. During the interview, I was asked how good I was at lying. I quickly indicated that I did not lie. The reply I received was a surprise. "Oh, that's a problem because in this business you have to lie. You won't get any business unless you are willing to lie!" My reply was simple. "Well, I am sorry, but I will not lie for you or for anyone, so I guess the job is not for me!" Upon which the interviewer said, "I guess you will become known as the honest trader." I got the job, and from day one my refusal to lie seemed to have little effect upon my ability to trade for the company. Even when we need a job, our Christian principles and conscience must take precedence. God takes care of the rest.

There are other times when our faith, and sometimes our friendship, is sorely tested. I am sure, like me, you have been approached to be complicit in someone else's dishonesty or fraudulent activity. This common dilemma arises when you are asked at work to sign in or sign out for someone who is not actually present. They want to leave early or arrive late and ask you to cover for them. You know they are defrauding the employer, and you have to make a judgment call. Then there are times when you are asked to sign papers as a witness or to put entries into forms which you know to be false. For instance, in making claims to insurance companies or filling out tax forms. To do so, you know you are lying as well as subjecting yourself to possible prosecution, but not to do so could cause the loss of a friendship. However, there is, on occasion, another surprising reaction. You might actually be respected for listening to your conscience, and the party in question could well refrain from doing what they had planned.

I know these are minor issues, but they are very real and do challenge our stand as Christians. Personal assaults upon our faith are harder to handle than the collective onslaught upon the church by the media. The media seizes every opportunity to decry, demean, or criticize the church and its ministry. Any mishap, mistake, or downfall of the clergy is highlighted to the detriment of the church's credibility, while the testimonies of changed lives are rarely mentioned. Governments are also not far behind the media by their muzzling of Christians on matters of doctrine and conscience. Has anything changed? Look at the early church and church history through the centuries. Opposition has been the order of the day. Where the church might become the conscience of society, society does not want to listen or heed the message given. The apostles, after their imprisonment and mistreatment, were forced to state, "We must obey God rather than men" (Acts 5:29). The church needs to take that same stand today.

WHAT IS THE ANSWER?

There is no answer or solution that will remove the opposition. However, there are answers that help us fight the battle against sin, and there are answers in helping us to face open opposition, but if our faith is real, then the opposition will always be with us. However, we need not be dismayed. There is hope and there is help. We are not left to fight alone.

FACING THE INTERNAL CHALLENGE

As new believers, we are called to "put off" the old life and "put on" the new. Paul outlines that responsibility with the words, "You were taught, with regard to your former way of life, to put off your old self, which is being corrupted by its deceitful desires, to be made new in the attitude of your minds; and to put on the new self, created to be like God in true righteousness and holiness" (Ephesians 4:22-24). We can take an active role by making choices to establish and improve our own spiritual growth, but as we consciously put off the old and put on the new and strive for holiness, so we become more aware of the struggle within.

We shall always experience temptation, but temptation is not sin. We will be offered the forbidden fruit and encouraged to participate, but we are promised the strength and grace to overcome. A comforting text from Scripture is "No temptation has seized you except what is common to man. And God is faithful; he will not let you be tempted beyond what you can bear. But when you are tempted, he will also provide a way out so that you can stand up under it" (1 Corinthians 10:13). What an incredible promise!

That escape route from temptation is provided by God through the ministry of his Spirit. Indwelt by the Holy Spirit, we are enabled to fight temptation. He it is who gives us the power to rise above it. Yet in the weakness of the flesh, we still give in to temptation and sin. It is at those times that we find consolation knowing that our sin, past and present, is covered by the Cross, and forgiveness is always available. John says, "If we claim to be without sin, we deceive ourselves and the truth is not in us. If we confess our sins, he is faithful and just and will forgive us our sins and purify us from all unrighteousness" (1 John 1:9).

As we recognize our sin, we need to confess and accept the love of God expressed to us through his forgiveness. Our life becomes one of continuous repentance and submission to God, his Word, and his way. All this comes to us through the ministry of the Spirit. We replace our previous master, sin, by the ultimate Master, Christ and his Spirit. Through salvation, God delivered us from the bondage and mastery of sin. As we seek to live supernaturally, we find ourselves gradually released from that prison of sin, freeing us from its domination and giving us freedom in Christ.

As the Spirit of God works in us and through us, he exudes his life. He allows us to enjoy the love, the peace, the joy, and all other aspects of his fruit. We will look more closely at the details of these spiritual characteristics as we progress. Suffice it to say here that it is only through the Holy Spirit that we can ever experience victory over sin and have the ability to express any spiritual qualities to others.

FACING THE EXTERNAL CHALLENGE

It is hard for me to talk about combating open opposition from a comfortable position of safety. This section should really be written by one who has gone through the fires of persecution. Yet, if our faith is real, then wherever we are and in whatever situation we find ourselves, our lives will be marked by spiritual warfare. For this we have been provided with the armor of God.

I know from personal experience that when you are in the army, you undertake the normal basic training, after which you are expected to move into active duty. You are expected to be prepared to move forward and, if necessary, to the front line, where you automatically engage the enemy. This is what you have been trained for: to gain ground and deplete the power of the enemy. The Christian life is the same. We are in a fight to gain ground—personally, as we gain ground moving forward by faith, and corporately, as we claim ground for the church. As believers, we are called to warfare.

Armor is made for protection; it is to defend ourselves. The sword is made for offense, to attack and fight. Paul wrote to Timothy, exhorting him to "Endure hardship with us like a good soldier of Christ Jesus" (2 Timothy 2:3). We are soldiers in spiritual warfare, whether we like it or not. Paul encourages us to "Put on the full armor of God so that you can take a stand against the devil's schemes" (Ephesians 6:11). An old adage says, "Know thy enemy," which is good advice for the believer when we read Paul's emphasis on the opposition. The struggle is real. It is against the powers of darkness and spiritual evil forces. The armor of God will protect us from potential, spiritual injuries and allow us to engage the enemy.

The Christian's spiritual life is a paradox because we are safe in the security of God's protection, and yet we are subject to the attacks of Satan. John Stott explains this when he says, "On the one hand, we are assured that, having been born of God, Christ keeps us safe 'and the evil one does not touch' us; on the other we are warned to watch out because the same evil one 'prowls around like a roaring lion looking for someone to devour.'"[3]

Some say that this passage of Scripture in Ephesians refers to human governments and authorities, while others major on the evil forces and principalities in the heavens. It can refer to both. The church receives opposition from earthly governments as well as direct opposition from demonic forces. Humans in any position, be it government or otherwise, are open to evil influence. Evil forces certainly distort the truth, resulting in false accusations against believers. The church receives constant opposition, both directly and indirectly. To deal with this, Paul tells us that "the weapons we fight with are not the weapons of this world. On the contrary, they have divine power to demolish strongholds" (2 Corinthians 10:4). We need to avail ourselves of the spiritual armor and weapons listed in Ephesians.

There are other good books that provide a full explanation of the armor of God, so I'll just briefly mention the list of armor pieces here. The spiritual armor pieces available to us are listed as the belt of truth, a breastplate of righteousness, feet fitted with the shoes of the gospel of peace, a shield of faith, and a helmet of salvation. The weapons given to us are the sword of the Spirit, which is the Word of God, and prayer in the Spirit. It is interesting to see the Spirit mentioned twice, providing effectiveness as he gives strength and power to the believer. The preparation is a conscious choice and action by the believer. As soldiers of Christ, it is imperative that we dress for battle. We are responsible for putting on the armor. How else can we stand? How else can we win?

We must not overlook that the Scripture says no matter what happens to us, we cannot be separated from the love of Christ even if we go through hardships, persecution, famine, or face the sword. Paul affirms this by declaring, "In all these things we are more than conquerors through him who loved us. For I am convinced that neither death nor life, neither angels or demons, neither the present or the future, nor any powers, neither height nor depth, nor anything else in creation, will be able to separate us from the love of God that is in Christ Jesus our Lord" (Romans 8:37-39). Someone once said that "we have to face death to look seriously at life."

Facing death has been common in the lives of many believers down through the years and up to the present time. In fact, it was reported that there were more Christian martyrs during the twentieth century than all the previous centuries combined. We are reminded of the familiar quotation, "The blood of the martyrs is the seed of the church." This certainly seems to prove itself when, during times of suffering, the church grows numerically and stronger spiritually. When the Chinese expelled foreign missionaries in 1947, they thought that would be the end of the Christian church. It only succeeded in driving the church underground, which has exploded in its growth to an estimated sixty million Christians.

Those who are faithful to God and proclaim the truth of God will face opposition. In the Old Testament we see Joseph mistreated, falsely accused, and falsely imprisoned yet placed by God into a strategic position where he could fulfill his purposes. Daniel was faithful in his devotion to God and was thrown into a den of lions, only to be rescued by God. Jeremiah also proclaimed the prophecies of God to his people. They rejected his message, and he was imprisoned down a well for his faithfulness. The New Testament is similar when it records that the apostles were flogged and jailed, Stephen was stoned, and Paul suffered extensively at the hands of accusers, all for preaching the gospel. Should we really be surprised at opposition to the Christian faith today? I think not.

Our call to action is boldness; not to think we can stand in our own strength but in the strength and power of the Holy Spirit. Paul brings comfort and assurance in his statement, "I consider that our present sufferings are not worth comparing with the glory that will be revealed in us" (Romans 8:18). Coming from someone who was beaten, stoned, imprisoned, and tortured, the statement is powerful and meaningful. Jesus, too, endorses the confidence that Christians can have under opposition when he said, "Blessed are you when people insult you, persecute you and falsely say all kinds of evil against you because of me. Rejoice and be glad, because great is your reward in heaven, for in the same way they persecuted the prophets who were before you" (Matthew 5:11-12). With such a confidence boost from Jesus himself, we should welcome insults to our faith. We should look for, and expect, such opposition, because if they treated Jesus that way, why should we be treated differently? We need to convey confidence and boldness as followers of Jesus.

Where do we go from here? Why should we accept hardships or opposition? What motivates us to live unashamedly expressing our faith? As we consider the spiritual dynamics and purpose in all of this, we will see what it is that drives us forward.

QUESTIONS FOR GROUP STUDY:
WHY IS THE CHRISTIAN LIFE SO DIFFICULT?
Reading: Ephesians 6:10–18

1. Is it true to say that life will always be difficult for the Christian? Explain your answer.

2. How much persecution do we really experience in the West?

3. What are the inward spiritual struggles we have to deal with?

4. Why is it that a believer constantly struggles to overcome sin and temptation?

5. Should we take comfort in the fact that all our sin, past, present, and future, has all been covered by Calvary? How does it affect us to know that?

6. How do we stop disappointment and discouragement from overwhelming us? What does it mean to live in the victory Jesus won for us on the cross?

8

WHAT THEN IS OUR MOTIVATION?

"For Christ's love compels us."
2 Corinthians 5:14

One Saturday morning when I was in the British Army, I left the camp where I was stationed—two hours prior to the authorized time on my pass. Under army rules that was going AWOL, which means *absent without leave*, a punishable offence. An officer discovered my absence. Consequently, on the following Monday morning I was marched between two camp military policemen to the office of the camp commandant to be charged with the offence. After hearing that I had completed the tasks set for me to do before I left camp, the commandant appeared to take a lenient attitude. Commending me for, in his own words, "working while you are here," he ordered I be confined to barracks for one month. This was the punishment for two hours' absence.

For other minor infractions, some friends in my unit were subjected to the hand-aching task of spending hours peeling potatoes from a pile that was taller than a man. The army was ingenious in finding humiliating ways of keeping you motivated to stay on track. One day I saw a soldier actually cutting grass on the base with a pair of scissors! In the army you are motivated to obey the rules and regulations by the threat of punishment, and generally it is effective.

Do you remember the times in your life when other people attempted to motivate you? Usually it begins with parents, then teachers, then college professors, and finally employers. Motivation is a good thing. It makes us recognize potential in ourselves and opportunities that we might never have considered possible. Motivation helps to get us out of our comfort zones. As we grow, we are generally motivated, or at least encouraged, to achieve higher marks, strive for a superior position, or earn that coveted promotion. These were probably good and maybe even the best for us, but unless we are motivated from within, other people can talk all day, but their words of encouragement will fall on deaf ears.

During the last several decades, motivational speaking has become a huge financial business. The purpose is to motivate people to realize their potential and achieve financial and business goals that they thought were not possible. For some it seems to work, while for others it makes little difference. However, motivation in life is important.

Living the Christian faith requires motivation. Other people can teach us, and we can willingly receive instruction with the best intention of implementing it, but until we have a genuine reason and motivation to live out the Christian life, very little will occur. It's necessary for us to hold conclusive reasons for walking the Christian pathway. It is important that when the road gets rough, we can fall back on the deep-seated reason why we made our commitment in the first place. It provides stability at those crucial times.

What is it that motivates us in our Christian walk? What impels us to serve our Master? What motivates us to render service to our King? What is it that keeps us motivated when the Christian life becomes hard and nothing seems to go right in our lives? What motivates us, when life and people are difficult, to rise above adversity? What keeps us going when we receive disappointment and discouragement? Without motivation, the Christian life can be very difficult. But before we look at motivation, let us just consider for a moment whether all obstacles we face are necessarily bad. Is there not a positive side to Christians facing adversity?

CAN HARDSHIPS EVER BRING BLESSING?

In our last chapter, we concentrated on the negative aspects of our internal struggle with temptation and the external opposition we face as believers. However, not all difficulties we experience are to our detriment. We have not mentioned unexpected trials, discouragements, disappointments, and other adversities that we inevitably face as we go through life. None of us are immune to the downside of life. Sickness and bereavement can hit us hard. On those occasions, it's difficult to imagine how anything good could come out of our situation and even more so, how the situation could ultimately work out for our own good. We have all been there, having had the same thoughts.

Paul's "thorn in the flesh" is familiar to us. Whatever it was, whether sickness, failing eyesight, or another ailment, is not clear, but three times he asked God to take it away. The answer was obviously "No." The word he received from God was, "My grace is sufficient for you, for my power is made perfect in weakness." So Paul went on to declare, "That is why, for Christ's sake I delight in weaknesses, in insults, in hardships, in persecution, in difficulties. For when I am weak, then I am strong" (2 Corinthians 12:9-10). It is hard to imagine anyone delighting in adverse situations, but Paul affirms this when he says, "I want to know Christ and the power of his resurrection and the fellowship of his sufferings, becoming like him in his death" (Philippians 3:10). He illustrates here the ultimate, the total sacrifice of self that is replaced by the life and death of Christ.

While everything is going well in our lives, we can easily accept and agree that difficulties might arise for our spiritual benefit, but at the time we are going through a depressive situation, fraught with disappointments, we rarely think it might be for our own good. At the time, it is virtually impossible to see any positive aspect and the potential good that may result—but it does happen, again and again.

As we walk the Christian path, our objective is to grow and progress in that walk. Often it is uphill. I understand that plants grow upright and strong because they have to push through the soil; otherwise, they would be weak, lifeless, and useless. It is the same for believers. We become strong as we are empowered by the Spirit of God to stand against obstacles. We mature in our spiritual walk as we willingly go through those situations that develop our Christian character

It would be most unusual if we enjoyed discipline, but discipline is necessary for us to grow spiritually. The writer to the Hebrews plainly states, "Endure hardship as discipline; God is treating you as sons. For what son is not disciplined by his father?" (Hebrews 12:7). Hardships can be God shaping our character; if so, then it has a purpose. That purpose is that we might develop, mature, and rise to new levels in our walk with God. Just as any child slowly develops by crawling, walking, and then running, our spiritual experience is similar, and adverse situations are often part of that experience.

One reason for hardships is to encourage us to trust more in God. As we face our own inability to do what we should do and to be what we should be, we learn about our inadequacy to do what is pleasing to God. We find ourselves forced to lean more and more on God. This is positive. We discover that God is faithful, true to his Word, and we find our relationship with him grows because of it. We are a work under construction. The Holy Spirit is building us up in our faith. As we read in Philippians "he who began a good work in you will carry it on to completion until the day of Jesus Christ" (Philippians 1:6). We rejoice in our conversion experience, but that is just the birth. We grow spiritually from that point on. Just like a baby has to be weaned, fed, and taught the ways of life, so the Christian cannot mature without going through the weaning process. Maturity always takes time. You have probably heard it said that "God hasn't finished with us yet." That will always be true.

The ultimate objective for the Christian is to reflect the image of Christ. That is a life-long process. It is a slow process of transformation. Sometimes hardships and difficulties play a real part in that spiritual exercise of change. We grow in our knowledge and understanding of the Christian faith. We cannot expect to learn overnight all that we need to know to walk successfully along the Christian path. We have to learn to walk before we can run. It calls for patience and diligence. The process has a name, which is *sanctification*. A big sounding word, maybe, but it simply means being separated or set apart for God's service. To achieve that end, we receive the "sanctifying work of the Holy Spirit" upon our lives as he guides, teaches, and shapes us toward being the people that God wants us to be.

When a potter takes a shapeless piece of clay and turns it into a beautiful vase, it has not been without much pummeling, twisting, turning, and shaping, until the potter is satisfied that the finished work is truly completed to his liking. The Christian's life is like that piece of clay. God the Holy Spirit works on us, shaping us and perfecting us into who we should be as followers of Jesus. Sanctification can also be likened to an artist painting on a canvas, God being the painter and we being the canvas. It takes a long time, layers and layers of paint, mistakes blotted out and reworked, until the artist is satisfied with the result. However, the work of God's Spirit in the life of the believer is never finished.

For the believer to take on the image of Christ is no simple task. The shaping and molding is carried out by the Holy Spirit. We cannot do it ourselves, even if we have the desire. Although there are choices we can make and disciplines we can choose that enable the Spirit to do his work, it is still his work. The process of sanctification can take many forms, some of which may be deliberate and painstaking and even painful. To deal with the sinful infection that has dictated our previous lives often creates a spiritual struggle and is never easy. Just as sickness in the natural body might call for a physical operation, so it is with the spiritual. It may call for some radical treatment to cut away habits and attitudes that have been resident for years. The change—and the healing—does not happen overnight. In fact, the duration of sanctification lasts the rest of our lives.

In Creation we were made in the image of God, but sin damaged that image. From the day of our conversion onward, we are being transformed into the image of Christ. As Paul explains it, "For those God foreknew he also predestined to be conformed to the likeness of his son" (Romans 8:29). He confirms it with "and we, who with unveiled faces all reflect the Lord's glory, are being transformed into his likeness with ever-increasing glory, which comes from the Lord, who is the Spirit" (2 Corinthians 3:18). To reflect the glory and image of Christ is to become Christlike. How we might wish it was an instantaneous transformation at the time of conversion! Unfortunately, this is not so. It is a growing process, and understandably so, because to be Christlike means to reflect his characteristics.

IS SUPERNATURAL TRANSFORMATION POSSIBLE?

God, in his wisdom, has provided for us the means whereby we can be transformed and conformed into his Son's image and portray his characteristics.

Whereas through the life and death of Jesus, salvation is made available, it is through the work and ministry of the Holy Spirit that we experience the work of progressive sanctification. The Holy Spirit brings regeneration, as we have seen, and in so doing, brings new life to the believer. He then maintains and develops that new life by providing spiritual nourishment and growth. His purpose is to bring the new believer to maturity in Christ. This development to maturity is called sanctification. It is progressive in that we are gradually released from the dominion and power of sin, while at the same time assuming the characteristics of Christ. This is exactly the purpose of the Spirit's work in the life of the believer: to make us more like Christ, to reflect his image, and to portray his holiness.

How is this possible? The Holy Spirit lives his life through the believer. His life is expressed in the believer, evidenced by the fruit and characteristics of the Holy Spirit that are identical to those of Christ. As the Christian portrays that fruit, so he displays those characteristics of Christ and begins to reflect his image. To fulfill our call to holiness is also dependent upon the ministry of God's Spirit in our lives. He alone can give us the spiritual ability to follow in the footsteps of our Master.

Natural fruit is the specific product relating to the particular plant, tree, or bush from which it is grown. Spiritual fruit in the life of the Christian pertains to, and is produced by, the indwelling Holy Spirit of God. This fruit is outlined for us in Paul's letter to Galatians where he says, "But the fruit of the Spirit is love, joy, peace, patience, kindness, goodness, faithfulness, gentleness and self-control" (Galatians 5:22). As we mature and progress in our walk, so this fruit is outwardly displayed. This is practical holiness in action. As the Spirit, who resides within us, is allowed to operate as he would choose, so our demeanor and behavior changes accordingly. We can now begin to see how the call to reflect Christ is more possible than we might have thought. The outward expression of that fruit exudes the very presence of Christ Jesus.

The Scripture refers to the fruit of the Spirit as singular. Someone has likened it to a cluster of grapes hanging from a vine: one bunch but different grapes. Just as John refers to Christ as the vine and we the branches, so the fruit hangs in clusters from the branches. The different aspects of the fruit are seen as Christian virtues and must be produced and depicted in the gracious spirit of the Lord. They are ineffective and unreal if produced in the flesh or by one's own efforts. It is only as we walk in step with the Spirit that the fruit can grow and become a dominant part of our life and character. The forthright instruction and explanation by Paul is readily understood. "Those who belong to Christ Jesus have crucified the sinful nature with its passions and desires. Since we live by the Spirit, let us keep in step with the Spirit" (Galatians 5:24-25). Our responsibility is to keep to the path, enabling the Spirit to do his work in us.

The purpose of the fruit in the believer is twofold. First, it is given for the spiritual walk and maturing of the Christian. It is for our spiritual well-being and our spiritual health. I also believe that this is part of the abundant life that Jesus promised for those who abide in him. Second, the outward display of these virtues expresses the reality of Christian faith and life. This is for the benefit of those who have no faith but are witnesses to its reality in our lives. The objective within the life of the believer is to bring glory to God. This will only be achieved as we reflect the image of Christ by displaying the fruit of the Spirit. As we do so, we live out the characteristics of Christ.

Our desire to do these things and live this way does not, in itself, remove the struggle to ensure success. Yet we are called to take deliberate steps to enhance such implementation. Dr J.I. Packer highlights this continuing struggle when he says, "Certainly God sometimes works wonders of sudden deliverance from this and that weakness at conversion, just as he does at other times; but every Christian's life is a constant fight against the pressures and pulls of the world, the flesh and the devil; and his battle for Christlikeness (that is, habits of wisdom, devotion, love, and righteousness) is as grueling as it is unending."[1]

To be Christlike is the objective before us, but it does not come without commitment and discipline. Although hardships are sometimes used to re-shape us, regrettably, we do not always bend the way we should. The fruit of the Spirit does not naturally occur in us. Our submission to God's Spirit will allow him to live out those spiritual characteristics through us.

So we, as Christians, have been given the armor of God to protect and defend ourselves against the enemy. We've been given the fruit of the God's Spirit to live a life that exemplifies a true follower of Jesus. When we express the love, joy, peace, and the other aspects of the fruit, then our lives are a testimony to the grace of God. In the next two chapters, we will look more closely at the fruit of the Spirit, but let me make this general observation at this point. Each different aspect of the fruit holds purpose within itself. For instance, the first three listed—love, joy, and peace—are all "states of being" for the believer. The second three—patience, kindness, and goodness—are expressions of the Christian faith worked out towards other people. The final three—faithfulness, gentleness, and self-control—are spiritual disciplines that, although they are basically inwardly applied, also testify to the reality and truth of the Christian life. The fruit of the Spirit is critical and imperative for us to achieve progress and effectiveness in our Christian lives.

WE ALL NEED MOTIVATION

We began the chapter by asking what it is that motivates us in our Christian living. What is it that enables us to stay the course, regardless of obstacles and opposition? There are two ways we can answer these questions. We can be motivated because of what we think God demands or expects from us, or by the fear of receiving his disapproval. On the other hand, we can be motivated by our response to him for that which we have already received. We daily receive the blessings of life through provision, protection, and care, which are all expressions of his love, but the greatest blessing is that we have received salvation. The result being that we are part of God's family and can respond to him as our father.

Fear, greed, and love are the greatest motivators in the world. Fear gets the adrenaline going and causes the fight or flight scenario. The fear of monetary loss or loss of possessions will cause us to create desperate measures to retain and preserve that which is ours. The fear of punishment or loss of privileges is another motivator for keeping us straight. Greed produces a slightly different reaction. It causes people to be devious and underhanded in order to benefit selfishly. It disregards principles and people in order to obtain its ends. Love is different again. Love for something or someone will invoke great sacrifice of time, energy, and money to satisfy a desire to please and enjoy. Love, for the Christian, must be the greatest motivator to serve and sacrifice.

We all have been recipients of God's eternal love. We have been the subjects of divine love from the Godhead. God expressed his love to us by sending his Son to identify with us in the flesh. Jesus expressed his love by giving his life to die on the cross for us. The Holy Spirit expresses his love by drawing us to Christ, by making us aware of salvation and performing the work of regeneration in our lives. For us to totally comprehend such love is virtually impossible, yet such love calls for a response.

Have you ever considered that the source of all love is God, for the Scripture says that "God is love" (1 John 4:8)? We could not even respond in love without God having first initiated his love in us. John says, "We love because he first loved us" (1 John 4:19). God's love forms the basis for our love back to him as well as our love for one another and our love for the world. In fact, the basis of all relationships in Christian theology is his love: within the Godhead, God to mankind, mankind to God, between believers, and Christians to the world. God's love is universal. It is sacrificial and unconditional. It is full of grace and mercy. God's love sanctifies, strengthens, and disciplines. Our love cannot compare, yet it is this love that God has placed within us. We are told, "God has poured out his love into our hearts by the Holy Spirit, whom he has given us" (Romans 5:5). With God's Spirit and God's love in our hearts, we are enabled to live the Christian life. It also provides our motivation for living life as a response to him.

We are indebted to Christ for his expression of unconditional love for us in dying on the cross. He gave his life in our place so that we might have true life in him. He redeemed us by paying the price for our release from the bondage of sin. To be purchased means new ownership. We now belong to him. Paul says, "You are not your own; you were bought at a price" (1Corinthians 6:19-20). God is our father and Christ our master. Our response to him has to be love and obedience. Charles Spurgeon once said, "Love is the mother of obedience: thus everything connected with our Lord lays us under obligation to obey him."[2] He was referring to the love of Christ, but the obligation becomes our privilege. We begin to get a glimpse of our motivation.

Although it is difficult, if not impossible, for us to comprehend the unconditional love of God, we can appreciate the extraordinary blessings we have received because of that love. Consequently, we find ourselves wanting to respond. The normal response is an overwhelming sense of thankfulness and gratitude to God. It also creates within us the desire to do what God wants us to do and be the person he wants us to be. Hence, it leads us to worship, devotion, and service, with that service based in love; unconditional, sacrificial and self-giving—the love that Christ had for us.

There is no greater motivation for Christian service than the recognition of God's love in Christ for us. God poured his love into our hearts for a reason. If we are inundated and overflowing with the love of God, as the Scriptures indicate, how can we not be outgoing with that love? The natural response is to express it and share it. We would then be fulfilling John's instruction that "since God so loved us, we also ought to love one another" (1 John 4:11).

When Jesus was questioned as to the greatest commandment, he replied, "Love the Lord your God with all your heart and with all your soul and with all your mind. This is the first and greatest commandment. And the second is like it: Love your neighbor as yourself" (Matthew 22:37). The expression of that love within us must be upward and outward. It has to be given back to God and then to those around us. In fact, it breaks into three segments: love to God, love to the church, and love to the world. We love God because he is our father. We love those within the church because they are our brothers and sisters; we love non-believers because we want them also to experience the love of God.

When all aspects of the fruit of the Spirit are listed (Galatians 5:22), love comes first. Some think that it is the main, and leading, facet of that fruit and even the source. There seems to be some element of truth in that, when you consider that most of the other aspects, such as kindness, goodness, and patience, need love to operate. Love is correctly referred to as the most important of Christian virtues.

CHRISTIAN LOVE IS THE ULTIMATE

When we talk about love in the Christian context, we are not referring to natural love or human love. That kind of love tends to be emotionally based, self-centered, and often conditional. Christian love is different. It is a product of the Holy Spirit and is therefore supernatural. It is an unusual love, it's an extraordinary love, and it goes far beyond natural love. It can only be exercised by those within the family of God, those who are born of the Spirit and indwelt by the Spirit of God. This real love is divine love, and it cannot be hidden. The proof of this love is displayed in our obedience to God and our love for others. William Barclay made a very good statement. He said, "More people have been brought into the church by the kindness of real Christian love than by all the theological arguments in the world."[3]

In our English language, we only have the one word for love. In the Greek language, there are four words for love. There is *eros,* which is sensual love between humans. This is the derivative of the word "erotic." Then there is *storge,* which expresses the love between family members. There is also *philia,* which carries the meaning of friendship love between people. The same word would be used for love of your country. From this root we get the word "philanthropy" and of course, the well-known city of Philadelphia (which means the city of brotherly love). Finally, we have the word *agape,* which is demonstrated in God's love to us and should be portrayed in our love to others. It is a love which is selfless and unconditional. We see this love expressed to us through the sacrifice of Christ on the cross. This is divine love. This is real Christian love.

Because the believer is indwelt by the Spirit of God, this divine love emanates from him. As it is displayed in our lives, it comes from the heart and the mind. It is not just an emotional response or a pleasant state of mind; its actions are by the will. We deliberately choose to love. We are called to love as the Father loves. God loves us regardless of our condition, background, or culture. We are instructed by Jesus to love our enemies. He says, "Love your enemies, and pray for those who persecute you" (Matthew 5:44). This is only possible through a supernatural love. It is only divine love that gives us the ability to love the unlovely and to love those who oppose us.

We have a friend who is a pastor in a large Romanian church. He related this story to us. He had a friend who was a well-known hymn-writer. His many songs are sung in the churches of Romania. This man had suffered over seventeen years in a Romanian prison because he would not write songs for the communist party. He was subjected to constant torture. Every time he was tortured, before it began, he would say to the torturer, "God loves you, and I love you, and I hope to see you in heaven one day!" The torture would then proceed.

Shortly after he was released from prison, this friend of ours had the occasion to visit him. The man opened the door with blood running down the side of his face. He said that his wound was the result of a visit from two secret police. He suggested our friend go in and that they should pray. As they got on their knees, our friend told us that he was so angry that he found it difficult to pray and could not remember what he said. Then the hymn-writer began to pray. He prayed for the men who had just beaten him. He prayed that they would hear and come to accept the gospel. Our friend was amazed and humbled as he listened to this man pray. His love was beyond understanding.

Not many weeks later, there was another knock on this man's door. When he answered, he was very disturbed to see his chief torturer standing at the door. His immediate thought was that the man had been sent to kill him. Apparently their tactic was always to send one man if there was to be a killing. Instead, the man said, "I have not come to harm you. Please, may I come in?" Once inside, he uttered these incredible words: "I have come to ask your forgiveness. Your love has won me over." He went on to say that he too wanted the faith that this man had, and he wanted to be on the same side. They knelt together and prayed, forgiveness was granted, and they parted as brother to brother. A short time later, the hymn-writer passed away.

This was no normal love. It was an incredible example of supernatural love. This man was certainly fulfilling the command of Jesus to "love your enemies." Such love is only possible by the presence and power of the Holy Spirit. It is true that few of us ever have to face such suffering for our faith, but we are called to display such an extraordinary love to others.

The New Testament treatise on love comes from 1 Corinthians 13. This is probably the most well-known and widely read passage on love, particularly used at wedding ceremonies. What is described here is the *agape* love and can only be experienced fully as fruit of the Spirit. When we read the main functions of this love, its attainment seems unreachable. We should attempt to memorize the central passage, "Love is patient, love is kind. It does not envy, it does not boast, it is not proud. It is not rude, it is not self-seeking, it is not easily angered, it keeps no record of wrongs. Love does not delight in evil but rejoices with the truth. It always protects, always trusts, always hopes, always perseveres" (1 Corinthians 13:4-7). This is the love of God, the love of Christ, and the love which emanates from the Holy Spirit.

Real Christian love does not come with pre-conditions, it has no hidden agenda, it is not self-seeking, and it does not demand power or position. It is patient and forgiving; it restores, it heals, and it unites. It is kind, compassionate, and generous without expecting a return. Christian love is humble, it acts responsibly, it is sensitive to others, and it never wants to be an obstacle or a spiritual stumbling block to others.

This chapter in Corinthians makes it plain that we might have everything this world has to offer, but without love, we have nothing. I read somewhere that he who does not love remains unblest, and he who lives without loving is just existing. We might even think we have a successful Christian life with all our involvement within the church, yet if our work is not carried out with love, we offer nothing. Love is Christian faith in action. If we have an overflow of God's love, how can we hide it? It will naturally overflow to others. Loving each other is the distinctive mark of the Christian. This is our calling. How do we shape up?

If we look at the early church, particularly in the Book of Acts, we see that love for one another was practical. It says that they had all things in common: They pooled their resources, sold possessions, and brought in the proceeds to share all things with all people. On this principle, there should be no poor or hungry within the church. We depend upon each other. Paul says in Romans 13 that we "belong to each other," which implies interdependence. Jesus left us instructions: "As I have loved you, so you must love one another" (John 13:34). Others rely upon us, and we rely upon them. Can others depend upon our love for them? We should be caring practically for one another. Do we share everything, or only out of what is left over?

Do we love unconditionally? Jesus loved us unconditionally. In fact, Jesus loved us while we were still in our sin. Do we have the right to place conditions upon our love? John even questions our love for God if we do not love our brother. He says, "For anyone who does not love his brother, whom he has seen, cannot love God, whom he has not seen. And he has given us this command: Whoever loves God must also love his brother" (1 John 4:20-21).

Loving our brother is the expression of Christ's love in us. This is all part of carrying the image of Christ. We reflect his characteristic of love. This is allowing the Holy Spirit to do his work and live through us. God loves others through us. Our preaching is not always pulpit preaching. Loving as Christ loved is living the gospel. Most of us know the words attributed to St Francis of Assisi: "Preach the gospel at all times and when necessary, use words." That should be us as we allow the love of Christ to touch the lives of others so that they, in turn, might respond to him.

God's love for us has to be the supreme motivator for living the Christian life. His love is the fountainhead of our spiritual being. Love is the foundation of the Christian faith. It involves God's love to us, our love to him, and then that love expressed to others. So, if love is the foundation, we need to build on that foundation. In the next two chapters, we will see how we build.

QUESTIONS FOR GROUP STUDY:

WHAT THEN IS OUR MOTIVATION?

Reading: 1 Corinthians 13

1. Are we motivated to walk the Christian life by God's demands or by our response to him?

2. As believers, what is our greatest motivator, and why?

3. What are the four different words for love in the New Testament? Explain the differences.

4. What do you understand as the real meaning of *agape*? Can we ever achieve that kind of love in our lives?

5. What is our reaction when we begin to comprehend the love of God for us?

6. How are we equipped to exercise the love of Christ?

QUESTIONS FOR GROUP STUDY

9

WHAT DO OUR FACES SHOW?

"We, who with unveiled faces all reflect the Lord's glory…"
2 Corinthians 3:14

Just as a picture is worth a thousand words, so faces tell a story. As a young boy growing up in England, I well remember the use of a common phrase, "You look as though you have lost a shilling and found a penny!" (A shilling was worth twelve pennies). Then there was another one, "Your face looks like thunder," suggesting black stormy clouds. Of course, everyone has heard the phrase, "You look as though you have seen a ghost!" In other words, our faces invariably show our inner feelings.

Then there are faces which depict a hard lived life. Sometimes a face matches the personality. Other times, one is surprised when it does not. I have heard it said of a person that they have a "lived in" face, which usually means the face has been ravaged with time. There are also soft faces portraying a gentle spirit and faces that show a pleasant disposition. Our face is the first aspect about us that creates an impression. It is an instrument of greeting. It is a bridge of communication to others. The shortest distance between two people is a smile.

It is hard for us to hide what is going on inside. Our spouses and others with whom we live can read our faces. How many times have you heard, "I can read you like a book!" When we receive bad news, disappointment, or discouragement, we find it difficult to hide our reactions. The same is true with good news—we find it difficult to hide our excitement and happiness. We grimace in pain. We laugh at good humor. Our approval or disapproval is also seen in our expression. Our faces reflect our lives.

For the Christian, our faces are often our badge of identification. How many times have you recognized another believer by their face and demeanor? In this chapter and the next, we will see why that is and why it should be. As we look at the various aspects of the fruit of the Spirit, we will see why we should be people who are recognized as being different.

THE FRUIT OF JOY

Joy is certainly something that should be reflected on our faces. We often mistake joy for happiness, but they are vastly different. Aristotle supposedly once said, "Happiness is the meaning and the purpose of life, the whole aim and end of human existence." If he did say that, then he was far off the mark. Happiness occurs from pleasurable circumstances. Happiness is not always present with us. It occurs and disappears determined by the activity of the moment.

When Kate Middleton emerged from Westminster Abbey after her marriage to Prince William and as they settled in the Landau that took them back to Buckingham Palace, we saw her say "I'm so happy" to her new husband. Could she be anything else but happy, having just married the future King of England and having moved from being Kate Middleton to being Catherine, the Duchess of Cambridge? Notice she said, "I'm so happy!" It was an emotional reaction to the outward circumstances in which she found herself. That's what happiness is, but joy is different.

Joy is a deep-rooted contentment in knowing that all is well, regardless of circumstance. It's like the deep water of the ocean. There might be a howling storm on the surface, but it makes little difference on the bottom of the ocean where all is calm. Christian joy is like that—a calm contentment that comes from knowing who is in control and that all will be well. It creates contentment, confidence, and assurance. The dictionary defines it as extreme gladness and a state of delight. Joy is an emotion, but a more stable emotion, and it produces an underlying stability in life.

In the Scriptures, joy is mentioned more than 150 times, as well as other words such as rejoice, delight, and gladness, which all come from the same Greek word *chara*. In the Old Testament, we see God's joy over his works and over his people. We see mankind rejoicing over the faithfulness of God. We see joy coming out of the relationship between God and his people. Just before the crucifixion and the ascension, Jesus emphasized that in spite of the fact that he was about to leave them, they would ultimately be filled with joy. Instructing them to follow his example by remaining in his love and obeying his commands, just as he had the Father's, Jesus says, "I have told you this so that my joy may be in you and that your joy may be complete" (John 15:11). Then, to emphasize the point, he says, "Now is your time of grief, but I will see you again and you will rejoice, and no one will take away your joy" (John 16:22). We see that promise of joy fulfilled in the lives of the apostles as they ministered in the early church.

The basis for the joy of the Christian is threefold. First of all, joy comes with the residence of the Holy Spirit in the believer, as joy is a fruit of the Spirit. Next, understanding the reality of salvation and the forgiveness we have received is cause enough for rejoicing and being joyful. Finally, the assurance of the eternal future with the Father is more than enough to fill the Christian's heart with joy. It was G.K. Chesterton who said, "Joy is the gigantic secret of the Christian." It is difficult for anyone to understand the joy of the Christian without having some understanding of salvation.

The Psalmist David talks about the joy of salvation, which is our experience as we begin to understand what salvation has brought to us, our privileged position in Christ, and our understanding of the grace of God. The Scriptures talk about an unspeakable joy that occurs within the believer. This is when we remember "from whence we came and where we are." We then experience the "joy of our salvation." Knowing we have been recipients of God's grace when we did not deserve it creates joy. We then recognize our gratefulness and thanksgiving as being so inadequate. Our standing in Christ, our daily blessings, and the future eternal prospect creates the foundation for our joy. Christians alone can experience such joy.

Joy is not just for those who have the right temperament. God's desire is that every member of his family enjoys and displays the fruit of joy. It is an expectation of the Christian. Paul says, "For the kingdom of God is not a matter of eating and drinking, but of righteousness, peace and joy in the Holy Spirit, because anyone who serves Christ in this way is pleasing to God and approved by men (Romans 14:17-18). We are expected to live in righteousness, peace, and joy, for this is pleasing to God. When Paul exhorts Christians to be "joyful always" (1 Thess 5:16), he is referring to the church as a community. He emphasizes the importance through repetition: "rejoice and again I say rejoice" (Philippians 4:4). So the church has a responsibility to be joyful and show that joy to the world. But are we always joyful? Do we ever lose our joy?

Many years ago I knew a young man who, at our Bible study group, insisted that—in his own words—"We are but worms!" His face was true to his belief. It is very disconcerting when you run into "joyless Christians." It causes you to ask the questions, where is the joy of the Lord, or where is the joy of salvation? Joyless Christianity has been called "practical atheism" because it denies who God is. It denies what he has done for us and overlooks his current care for us. The blessings of salvation and the blessings of every day are sadly ignored. There are times we should choose to rejoice because of what we know, regardless of what we see or feel. But, being realistic, undoubtedly obstacles and hindrances exist that interrupt our outward expression of joy.

As we experience the nearness and presence of God, we enjoy the delights of real Christian joy, but when that fellowship or relationship is disturbed, so is the joy. Sin in our lives will cause us to lose God's joy, not because God has moved away from us, but because we have become disappointed with ourselves and have broken the fellowship of his presence. Our joy then becomes diminished and repressed. David cried out to God, "Restore unto me the joy of your salvation" when he was seeking forgiveness for his sin of adultery.

Sin that we might consider small and insignificant can become hindrances to our joy as much as adultery was to David. Sins of the mind and attitude that are inconsistent with our walk with him are often the culprits. If we harbor a critical spirit, resentment, jealousy, lack of forgiveness, bitterness, envy, or spreading gossip—any of these things can take away the joy of the Holy Spirit. Joy and sin are incompatible: like water and oil, they do not mix. We may put on some pretense for a time, but ultimately the truth will surface. We soon discover that our sin is not only unbecoming of the character of the Holy Spirit, it is grievous to him.

Without a doubt, trials and troubles also dampen our joy until we are able to get God's perspective on our life. James says, "Consider it pure joy, my brothers, whenever you face trials of many kinds" (James 1:2). We have already seen how trials help us to grow spiritually. Once we regain the assurance that God still cares and is still in control, then gradually the joy is restored. We could say that it never left but was buried under the weight of our trial. Although the full implications of this phrase are not easy to understand, it was Spurgeon who said, "There is sweet joy which comes to us through sorrow." In the Scriptures we see that, in spite of the terrible state of their homeland when the children of Israel returned from their captivity in Babylon, they still rejoiced and were singing songs of joy. It says, "Our mouths were filled with laughter and our tongues with songs of joy" (Psalm 126:2). They considered their freedom and blessings were greater than the obstacles they faced in the situation around them.

This is also true for the believer today. When we understand from what we have been saved and the privilege we have as children of God, then joy supersedes any problems we might encounter. The spiritual overcomes the natural. We experience joy because we are secure in, and are upheld by, the love of God. We enjoy a confidence in our relationship with him. We have joy because we walk with God and enjoy his fellowship.

As the power of the Holy Spirit operates within us, and as we give him freedom to reign, we will experience his joy as one aspect of his fruit. Joy in our lives is a witness to the world. It is a badge of distinction. It demonstrates where we place our trust. It certainly is not in money or possessions or anything else. It is squarely on our position in Christ, our hope in Christ, and the certainty of God's sovereignty. We are exhorted to "rejoice in the Lord always" (Philippians 4:4). As we do so, joy as a fruit of the Spirit will be present with us.

THE FRUIT OF PEACE

There is an enormous desire for peace in the world—not just between countries but within the human heart. People seek to unload themselves of turmoil and conflict. The breakdown of relationships is common today, in marriages, in corporations, among governments, among friends and, yes, even between Christians. These situations create unrest and eradicate the presence of peace.

What is peace? Is it just the absence of conflict? If we go to the dictionary, the definition we find is "quiet, tranquility, calmness of mind, and serenity." This is the objective sought by the many thousands of people who have turned to meditation. They want to experience a peace and a calmness that will help them handle the stressfulness of life in business and in their personal lives.

In the New Testament, the Greek word for peace is *eirene*. This is the word from which we get the name of Irene, who was the goddess of peace. In the Old Testament, peace is depicted by the word *shalom*, which is used as a greeting. In the Jewish tradition, the word holds a sense of freedom from strife. It also conveys the meaning of wellness, the complete harmony of body, soul, and spirit. In the New Testament, peace is added to the greeting of grace, with "grace and peace to you" (Philippians 1:2). The greeting within the Anglican community is often referred to as "The Peace."

Spiritually, peace is based upon an unshakable confidence in God. This produces a deep-seated tranquility and calmness in all circumstances. It is a peace that is described in Scripture as something that cannot be comprehended; it goes beyond normal, natural understanding. Paul encourages us, "Do not be anxious about anything, but in everything, by prayer and petition, with thanksgiving, present your requests to God. And the peace of God, which transcends all understanding, will guard your hearts and minds in Christ Jesus" (Philippians 4:6-7). This peace is not man-made. It is a supernatural peace, one which brings protection like being within a fortress during an invasion. It is impossible for it to be humanly created, because it comes from God.

It is amazing how much we see joy and peace linked together in the Scriptures. What was it that the angels announced to the shepherds? They heard the words "Tidings of great joy to all people" and a message of "peace on earth." Paul says in Romans, "May the God of hope fill you with all joy and peace" (Romans 15:13). The close affiliation between the two makes sense because, if you are joyful, you are probably at peace, and if you enjoy peace, then you are likely to be joyful. Joy and peace go together. They are intertwined. There can be no peace without knowing Christ and no joy without the peace of God within the heart.

We cannot enjoy a peace of heart without first establishing a relationship with God. Peace with God means that our relationship with him is real through the forgiveness we received through redemption. The rift has been healed. The gap has been bridged through salvation, and we enjoy a harmony in fellowship with God. The receiving of this peace within the heart is one of the first experiences of those who come to faith in Christ. It is a peace that they have never experienced before, a peace that is virtually inexplicable. This is the supernatural peace of God. But it has only been made available to us through the Lord Jesus Christ. Paul says, "Therefore since we have been justified through faith, we have peace with God through our Lord Jesus Christ" (Romans 5:1). Christ came as the Prince of Peace and promised us his peace with the words, "Peace I leave with you: my peace I give you" (John 14:27).

As we have seen earlier in the book, it was through Christ's death that he took our punishment, our debt was paid, and God's justice was satisfied. So it was through the sacrifice of Christ that we can now experience peace with God. Our relationship with him is established and clear of any encumbrance of sin. The Cross of Christ is inextricably linked to our peace with God. This is highlighted in Colossians where we read, "through him to reconcile all things…by making peace through his blood, shed on the cross" (Colossians 1:20). We tend to avoid talking about the blood of Jesus today, but its critical aspect and the importance of it to salvation cannot be ignored. Peter emphasized its importance when he stated, "For you know that it was not with perishable things such as silver or gold that you were redeemed from the empty way of life handed down to you from your forefathers, but with the precious blood of Christ, a lamb without blemish or defect" (1 Peter 1:18-19).

It was Edward Henry Bickerseth who wrote the following words early in the nineteenth century, which are still sung today:

> *Peace perfect peace in this dark world of sin?*
> *The blood of Jesus whispers peace within.*

Archaic it may sound, but its truth is still relevant, that real peace can only be realized through the sacrifice of Christ.

The peace of God as a fruit of the Spirit is displayed in the life of the Christian as a serenity, a calmness, and a peacefulness because of an underlying confidence in God. In the Authorized Version of the Scripture, God says to the children of Israel, "In quietness and confidence shall be my strength" (Isaiah 30:15). It gives the picture of a quiet calmness through confidence in God the Father. We look at a perfectly still lake and mention how peaceful it is. We, as Christians, should portray a similar quietness and calmness brought on by our confidence in the sovereignty of our God. Such a peace proves to be the Christian's strength in a world of turmoil. We need to walk in the truth of God's sovereignty, acknowledging that he is in control of all things. If our minds are fixed on God, then he grants to us his peace. God's Word gives us this promise: "You will keep in perfect peace him whose mind is steadfast because he trusts in you" (Isaiah 26:3).

Christian peace provides security. It causes us not to panic, even in times of anxiety, financial or family problems, unemployment, or ill health. Everybody suffers disappointments, relational problems, and frustrations, but we are reminded of the little bird that, while the raging storm goes on, sits quietly and securely in the crevice of a rock. As Christians, our experience in life should be like that. Amid the rough patches of life, we can know and experience the peace of Christ. As God is our Father, so we will remain in peace as we stay in his presence.

I read a story about a Lutheran missionary who, along with a number of other missionaries, was on a ship crossing the Atlantic during

WWII—returning home. Their ship was torpedoed by the Germans. They were picked up by the same German vessel; the men and women were separated and put into different holds of the ship for sleeping. In the morning they were allowed to be together and talked about the night. One missionary said he had thought he would not sleep because of the conditions. They were prisoners of war and in the hands of the enemy. The conditions were stark and uncomfortable. They were expected to sleep on a hard, cold floor. But he did sleep. He said that when he laid down, words from Psalm 121 came to mind. "My help cometh from the Lord...He that keepeth thee ... will neither slumber nor sleep" (Authorized Version). He became confident by the truth of these words and said, "Lord, there really isn't any point in both of us staying awake. If you are going to keep watch, then I would be grateful for some sleep." He slept soundly. He experienced peace in a situation where it was least expected.

Just as with joy, our peace can also be disturbed. There are a many things that might cause this: misunderstanding, disunity, dysfunctional relationships, sin, disobedience, a lack of forgiveness, frustration, and crises. We are human and we live in a fallen world, so even with our God-relationship intact, we can still suffer from disturbing situations and adversity. It is difficult for peace and worry to exist together; one has to give way to the other. At those times, we are called to follow Peter's advice to "Cast all your anxiety on him because he cares for you" (1 Peter 5:7). This is easier to say than to do. Even when we choose to do so, we have a tendency to take the anxiety away with us. We ask ourselves, is God sovereign? Is he in control in all circumstances? If he is, then we can trust him implicitly in whatever situation we find ourselves. He doesn't always remove the obstacle or change the circumstances we face, but he promises peace to see us through.

As Christians, our responsibility is to display the fruit of the Spirit, which includes this aspect of peace. This is where our faces and our actions can tell the story. Because we are indwelt by the Spirit of God and peace is part of his character, so it should be ours and will be reflected outwardly to others. As we mix with neighbors, colleagues, friends, and those within the family of God, it should be evident that we are at peace with God, with them, with ourselves, and with those within the church. This is one area where our faces, our behavior, and our deportment demonstrate the peace within. This is all part of bearing the image of Christ. More than just a responsibility, we should have the desire to live at peace with all men as encouraged by the writer of Hebrews who says, "Make every effort to live in peace with all men" (Hebrews 12:14). These are very similar to Paul's words: "Make every effort to keep the unity of the Spirit through the bond of peace" (Ephesians 4:3). The words of Jesus, "Blessed are the peacemakers" (Matthew 5:9), remind us of the line in the song we sing, "Let there be peace on earth and let it begin with me." We should contemplate how we can implement that principle.

We are, and always will be, dependent upon the Holy Spirit and his work to produce peace as part of his fruit within us. It is not only for our own spiritual benefit but for the benefit of the church. We enjoy cordial friendship and true fellowship as we serve together in the unity of peace. The witness, the testimony, and the credibility of the church are at stake. Discord and disunity are in opposition to the fruit of the Spirit. We are a spiritual community. We are one body. We may be many parts, but we are all equal in service. We are interdependent, and by working together in peace, we create one purpose, one sense of vision, and one goal of achievement, which is to bring glory to God in our lives and in the church.

THE FRUIT OF PATIENCE

Margaret Thatcher, when she was prime minister of the United Kingdom, once said, "I am extraordinarily patient, provided I get my own way in the end!" We have all heard this prayer, "Give me patience,

Lord, but hurry up about it." Probably Philip Brooks had a better understanding when he said, "I'm in a hurry, but God isn't!"

Patience is the ability to endure delay, hardship, and provocation. It also implies perseverance. In the New Testament, the Greek word *makrothymia* is interpreted as longsuffering, forbearance towards others, perseverance, and endurance. Patience has been called the passive but tenacious side of love, while kindness is referred to as having the active role. We read that "love is patient" (1 Corinthians 13:4). Patience finds its basis in love. They are closely linked together. Patience is love displayed. The character and nature of Christ is reflected in the fruit of the Spirit. This includes patience, which Paul exhorts his readers to "put on" as one of many Christian virtues. He says, "Therefore, as God's chosen people, holy and dearly loved, clothe yourselves with compassion, kindness, humility, gentleness and patience" (Colossians 3:12). This is all part of taking off the old self and putting on the "new self, which is being renewed in knowledge in the image of its Creator" (Colossians 3:10). We are called to godly patience as we seek to reflect the image of Christ.

Jesus received ridicule, open hostility, devious opposition, and undeserved criticism, yet he demonstrated patience with all his enemies. He was patient with his disciples, with the Pharisees, the Sadducees, and non-believers. We read that "when they hurled their insults at him, he did not retaliate; when he suffered, he made no threats. Instead, he entrusted himself to him who judges justly" (1 Peter 2:23). We wonder how we would react under similar mental strain and stress. Reaction might be our answer, but response is a sign of patience, and Jesus certainly did that. His example is our aim.

When we suffer abuse and mistreatment, we find it difficult to return patience and forbearance instead of bitterness and resentment. We get frustrated and annoyed when we suffer aggravation and consider our grievance is justified. This kind of situation was not uncommon in the New Testament church for we see, spelled out for us, the antidote to our anger and our reactions of rage that lead to provocation. It is, says Paul, "that you may live a life worthy of the Lord and may please him in every way: bearing fruit in every good work, growing in the knowledge of God, being strengthened with all power according to his glorious might so that you may have great endurance and patience" (Colossians 1:10-11). We readily admit our need for patience when we are upset and hurt.

If you have ever been ridiculed for your faith or had your Christian principles demeaned, patience is not the first thing that comes to mind. If you have been unjustly accused of wrongdoing, which is most difficult to handle, or you have been misunderstood even when your intentions were nothing but good, your reaction is normally an urgent need to set the record straight and let the truth be known. In the workplace, Christians can be subject to corporate intrigue or unfair management practices. Even in the home, there can be unexpected and harsh opposition or criticism from those who do not believe the same. All these situations call for God-given patience, forbearance, and a longsuffering attitude.

We need to be gracious about the faults of others because we too have faults of our own. This calls for humility. Hear what Paul says: "Be completely humble and gentle; be patient, bearing with one another in love" (Ephesians 4:2). Forbearance and forgiveness are also closely aligned. Colossians tells us to "bear with each other and forgive whatever grievances you may have against one another. Forgive as the Lord forgave you" (Colossians 3:13). To do so, we must exercise patience motivated by love. If we think more highly of ourselves than others, then our patience will be condescending. This is not Christlike. We must look at people and situations through the compassionate eyes of God. Then our patience will be formed and exercised in love.

How we handle frustrating and annoying situations will often be equal to our confidence in God and who he is. We can rest assured that he knows all and knows best. We have the assurance that God will bring proper justice in his time. It may not be our time, but certainly in his. The Scripture makes it plain that "God is just: He will pay back trouble to those who trouble you and give relief to you who are troubled" (2 Thessalonians 1:6). It is wise to always remember that God knows the truth and his justice is perfect.

God is a God who is patient. We read that the Lord is "the compassionate and gracious God, slow to anger, abounding in love and faithfulness, maintaining love to thousands, and forgiving wickedness, rebellion and sin" (Exodus 34:6-7). God's patience was extraordinary with his people Israel, as he forgave them again and again for their obstinate rebellion. God's patience is extraordinary for all people as they stand against him in arrogance, rebellion, and the rejection of his love. When Paul paints a picture of humankind, he asks an appropriate question regarding this obstinacy. His question is "do you show contempt for the riches of his kindness, tolerance and patience, not realizing that God's kindness leads you to repentance?" (Romans 2:4). And repentance, we all know, is a prerequisite for a relationship with God. We enjoy salvation because God was patient with us. How can we not be patient with others?

We have Job as an example of patience as well as the many thousands through the centuries who have patiently accepted their suffering for their faith. Christian patience is not submission to our situation; it is submitting to the knowledge that God will overrule in the end. Patience is a gift of God. It is part of the fruit of the Spirit. It is a characteristic of Christ. Like the rest of the fruit of the Spirit, patience is not an optional extra for the Christian life; it is essential. We must take steps to "put on patience," yet we cannot produce it without the working of the Holy Spirit in our lives. Patience is an important virtue. It comes to us only by the grace of God and through the indwelling Holy Spirit.

Abraham Kuyper, the Dutch theologian and one time prime minister of the Netherlands, once said, "Patience is a strength of spirit, engendered within the heart of God's children by the Holy Spirit, which enables them to remain standing, unshaken and undaunted, in spite of all the forces that would tear them from the Kingdom of God."

THE FRUIT OF KINDNESS

I know a lady whom everyone would classify as being kind. Although not young herself, she quickly picks up on the needs of others. She transports people to hospitals to visit spouses. She ensures that they have food in the house. She has an incapacitated relative stay with her a few days at a time to give a break to those permanently caring for the person. She is at the time in life when most people would need assistance, yet she is always serving others. This lady does not have to do what she is doing, but that is the nature of kindness: it is meeting the needs of others without expecting a return.

Unlike joy, peace, and patience, which are inner states of being, kindness is recognized in its outward expression. It is not just an attitude of heart. It is behavior that is motivated by love. Kindness is recognized as being friendly, being generous, and showing benevolence. We consider people to be kind by their manner, their kindly attitude, their helpfulness, their empathy, and their understanding, resulting in kind acts.

In Scripture, the story of the Good Samaritan is one with which we associate kindness. In the story it was assumed that this was a Jewish man going down to Jericho, and normally the Jews had no dealings with the Samaritans; in fact, they despised them and would not normally associate with them. But here was a Samaritan being kind to a Jew. If this Jew held the normal anti-Samaritan attitude, did he deserve the treatment he received? Kindness sometimes means loving people more than they deserve. Kindness is a matter of the will. The Samaritan overlooked the attitude because he saw someone in need. The need for us to show kindness will derive from the Holy Spirit causing the awareness. We will find ourselves responding when it is inconvenient and going into uncomfortable situations even where we would rather step back and walk away.

Kindness is an attitude which results in kind action. This can be a simple action of a smile or the recognition of anyone who provides you with a service such as a sales person, a waiter, a police officer, or any other person with whom you have a passing contact. It means telling people they are doing a good job, especially when their task appears to be trivial or demeaning. Kindness is an expression of Christ's character to people through his followers.

We have no idea how many people need our ministration of grace, mercy, and kindness. We represent Christ. We seek to bear his image. We are the hands and feet of Jesus to this hurting world. Kindness is being sensitive to the needs of others and then seeking to do something practical to meet those needs. This also aligns very much with goodness, another aspect of the fruit of the Spirit at which we will look in the next chapter.

Needs of people are varied, and we must be sensitive to them. In linking patience with kindness, Gordon Fee says, "If longsuffering means not to chew someone's head off, kindness means to find ways of binding up their wounds."[1] Giving practical help, emotional support, and particularly meeting spiritual needs requires the investment of time and effort. It calls for proper counsel, sensitivity, understanding, and love. People recognize genuine kindness because their interest is taking precedence. It portrays Christian character.

God's kindness is the basis of our kindness. Kindness is part of the character and nature of the Trinity. As we submit to the Holy Spirit and seek to bear his fruit, then kindness will become part of our nature. We are recipients of salvation through the kindness of God shown to us through his grace and through the Lord Jesus Christ. We read in Titus that "when the kindness of God and love of God our Savior appeared, he saved us, not because of righteous things we had done, but because of his mercy" (Titus 3:4-5). Likewise, Paul reiterates the same when he says, "And God raised us up with Christ and seated us with him in the heavenly realms in Christ Jesus, in order that in the coming ages he might show the incomparable riches of his grace, expressed in his kindness in Christ Jesus" (Ephesians 2:6-7). Such blessing leaves us no alternative but to share, and not only to those who love us or are kind to us, but to those who deliberately provoke us. Jesus gave us instructions: "But love your enemies, do good to them, and lend to them without expecting to get anything back" (Luke 6:35). That is genuine kindness. It is to such kindness that we are called.

QUESTIONS FOR GROUP STUDY
WHAT DO OUR FACES SHOW?
Reading: Galatians 5:13-26

1. What do you understand as the difference between happiness and joy?

2. Is it really possible to have joy even when going through trials and difficulties? Explain your reasoning.

3. What is the Christian's peace based upon?

4. What kinds of things or events disturb our peace? Is it possible to retain peace during turmoil and even conflict? If so, how?

5. How can we be tolerant and patient in annoying and frustrating situations? Is there ever a situation where anger is right?

6. In a society which is "me" centered, has kindness become a forgotten characteristic? How can Christians counteract this situation?

10

WHAT IS PORTRAYED BY OUR ATTITUDE?

"Your attitude should be the same as that of Christ Jesus."
PHILIPPIANS 2:5

In my younger days, I worked in a London office where the supervisor had an atrocious attitude. He was miserable from the time he walked into the office to the time he left. His comments throughout the day were negative, and he could not say anything good about the job, the employers, or even life in general. I often wondered what his home life was like. The sad thing was that his attitude affected the atmosphere of the office. It was virtually unacceptable to be positive and happy. It was like walking into a big black cloud every morning. Needless to say, I did not stay around long.

We have all heard the statement "He has a bad attitude" or its opposite "He has a good attitude about it," usually referring to someone who has reacted well to an unfortunate experience or someone who is trying to make good out of a bad situation. Whether for good or bad, attitudes have an influence, and Christians are not exempt. In fact, the Christian carries an added responsibility to demonstrate or respond in life with a good attitude.

A person's character is reflected in his or her attitude. A serious flaw in our character will show up in our attitude, both to life and to others.

Our character is shaped and formulated by many influences in life: our parents, our home life, our education, our peers, and all we assimilate as we grow. For the Christian, our character development is influenced by our Christian faith, and no more so than by the fruit of the Spirit evidenced in our lives. So let's consider goodness, faithfulness, gentleness, and self-control as they affect our lives, our attitude, and our character.

THE FRUIT OF GOODNESS

Patience is considered to be the passive side of Christian character because it is not an overt outward expression. Kindness is the active side because it can be seen within the nature of a person, while goodness is the practical outworking of kindness. Thus kindness and goodness are closely entwined. But how do we see the fruit of goodness? It appears to be a relative term that needs a context to determine its meaning. The word *good* is used in many different ways. You can be good at study, you can have good brakes on your vehicle, you can have good eyesight, and you can be good at sport. We say, "Good morning," or "It is a good day." The word carries diverse meanings. It can mean commendable, reliable, admirable, enjoyable, kind, noble, and upright. It can also carry the meaning of being moral or of good character. Someone once said that "goodness is easier to recognize than define." Yet the word *good* is subjective to the user because what is good to you might not be good to me, as evidenced by book and film reviews. Thus the words *good* and *goodness* usually take their meaning from the context. Remember how it was always difficult to understand when your parents said, "This is for your own good!" which was usually accompanied by some deserved punishment?

The expression of goodness in the life of the believer is not "being good" for the sake of appearing to be good. This is not about being good, but doing good. Jesus went about doing good among the people. He healed the sick; he touched their bodies and changed their lives. He fed the hungry, and he comforted those who mourned. His goodness expressed his compassion. As followers of Jesus, our goodness should also express the love of Christ in us. His love must always be the motivation and the foundation for the good we seek to do.

As Christians, we are called to goodness, but that goodness is based upon the goodness of God. What would our motive be if we were not influenced by the Spirit of God? We are called to "share with God's people who are in need" and to "practice hospitality" (Romans 12:13). Paul outlines the attitude and disposition of a Christian leader, which includes being hospitable, loving what is good, being self-controlled, upright, holy, and disciplined (Titus 1:8). Referring to believers as being salt of the earth and the light of the world, Jesus calls the believer to a practical outworking of that light when he says, "let your light shine before men, that they may see your good deeds and praise our Father in heaven" (Matthew 5:16).

How many times have you heard it said that "God is good"? That is because he is. God abounds in goodness expressed in his compassion, his graciousness, and his love. God is the source of all good. Jesus said, "no one is good except God" (Luke 18:19). Just as we indicate that God is love, so we describe his character when we say that God is good. We are recipients of that goodness; therefore, as it is enacted in our lives, we reflect the goodness of God. Paul commends the Christians in Rome for being "full of goodness" (Romans 15:14).

One astounding passage of Scripture places our call to do good works in real perspective. We read, "For we are God's workmanship, created in Christ Jesus to do good works, which God prepared in advance for us to do" (Ephesians 2:10). Our relationship with God through Christ has been established that we might do good works. Salvation is not just for our spiritual satisfaction or security. It is also not provided for us to sit back and enjoy the benefits and privileges of being in the family of God. We are called to work and serve. What's more, our good works have already been pre-planned by God. Our responsibility is to determine what it is we are to do. It is awesome and somewhat apprehensive to think that, in God's sovereignty, he already has a plan worked out for us.

God has created us, and as long as we remain submitted to him, he will make us into the people he wants us to be. He gives us the gifting and abilities to carry out the works he has chosen for us. He has given us his Spirit that we might be strengthened by his grace to serve and work in the kingdom. His Spirit gives us guidance as to where we should serve, what we should do, and how we should do it. It is our duty to be sensitive to the direction of God's Holy Spirit. The purpose of good works is always that God might be glorified. We are called to "Live as children of light (for the fruit of light consists in all goodness, righteousness and truth) and find out what pleases the Lord" (Ephesians 5:9-10).

How then might this goodness be seen in us? It is interesting that in the New Testament, Barnabas is called "a good man, full of the Holy Spirit and faith" (Acts 11:24), and we see Dorcas referred to as a "good" woman for all her charitable work caring for the poor. Barnabas had a wonderful attitude and encouraged people in the faith. His goodness was seen in how he treated people, while the goodness of Dorcas was seen in her practical assistance to those in need. So how then should our goodness be expressed? I believe it should be in the same way; in our attitude to others and in seeking practical ways to minister and change someone's life for the better.

The fruit of goodness can be expressed in an act of generosity, perhaps even sacrificial giving. It might be in the exercise of "going the extra mile" and giving time and extra effort where you can ill afford it, being motivated to go beyond what might be expected of us. Goodness will be seen in our thoughtfulness, our sympathy and empathy expressed in our attitude to others, our unselfishness, as well as our tolerance and a readiness to forgive. We see in the New Testament church that even the widow was expected to fulfill a role in "helping those in trouble and devoting herself to all kinds of good deeds" (1 Timothy 5:10). Although a normal and natural responsibility, caring for those within the family was an expression of goodness and was expected.

Goodness is an act to be exercised inside and outside the church. We are called to do good to all people, but we have a special responsibility towards those within the family of God. We read, "Therefore, as we have opportunity, let us do good to all people, especially those who belong to the family of believers" (Galatians 6:10). During the harsh days of communistic rule in the Soviet Union, as it was then known, many pastors were jailed because of their faith and their spiritual leadership. It was the custom of the government to deny all further State benefits to the families of those prisoners. Scores of families were made destitute by such action, and it was to these people that fellow believers became the source of economic survival. They cared well for these suffering families. This was just one example where the church put Scripture into action by doing good deeds for their brothers and sisters. It should still be a high priority within the church today.

As members of the church universal, we are all part of the body of Christ. We are closely linked together, we fit together, we are interdependent, and we belong to each other. As one member suffers, so all should feel the pain. As another rejoices, so all should delight in the blessing. Our attitude of love and unity should naturally result in doing good for fellow members.

The fruit of goodness should also be a blessing to those who are outside the church. We are encouraged to "not become weary in doing good, for at the proper time we will reap a harvest if we do not give up" (Galatians 6:9). N.T. Wright, in his book *After You Believe*, highlights the fact that those who step up to the plate to perform acts of kindness and goodness within the community come primarily from the church. He states, "In England, the government's own statistics show that the solid majority of those who give of their time, money, and energy to voluntary service in their communities—working with the elderly, the handicapped, the dying, the very young and so on—are practicing Christians. Many of them would say that they're not very good Christians....But something in the lifeblood of the church has stirred them to offer help where help is needed, and they do it gladly, finding (not surprisingly) such a strong personal fulfillment in doing so that it keeps them coming back even when they themselves are getting old and tired."[1] I can personally attest to that last fact. My own parents would in their own words "serve coffee to the old people on Saturday mornings" when they themselves were into their mid-eighties.

Christians are called to action by putting into practice this aspect of the fruit of the Spirit. We read, "Each one should use whatever gift he has received to serve others, faithfully administering God's grace in its various forms" (1 Peter 4:10). We must learn what it means for us individually to do good—to live goodly lives as well as godly lives. We must learn to be sensitive to the needs of others so that we might readily offer help. Some things we do will be unseen, unrecognized, and unheralded. Our actions should not be for that purpose. It does not matter that we might operate in the background and never be in the limelight. Our motives must be right. We must serve for the blessing of others, not self-centeredly, but with the objective that God might be glorified.

I believe one of the saddest lines in the Psalms is when David says "No one cares about my life" (Psalm 142:4). This should never be the indictment against us as believers. Jesus said, "The good man brings good things out of the good stored up in his heart" (Luke 6:45). When we see the need, we must act. In doing so, we are applying the character of Christ through his goodness into that situation. Our actions should depict our faith. The resident Holy Spirit should be evident, and our actions should express the love of Christ.

THE FRUIT OF FAITHFULNESS

Faith is both a fruit of the Spirit and a gift of the Spirit. Where Paul in his epistle to the Galatians listed the fruit of the Spirit, several translations now use the word faithfulness. The gift of faith is often evidenced in one-off situations where the act of faith is required. It is mostly given for specific circumstances and at a specific time, whereas the fruit of faithfulness can be operative in the life of a believer day in and day out.

The gift of faith is necessary for salvation. It is implanted within the believer for that very reason. It is also the basis for our on-going faith as we walk the Christian life. The Scripture indicates that "the just shall live by faith" as opposed to law and legalism. It states that we, as believers, live by faith and not by sight (2 Corinthians 5:7). "Sight is not faith, and hearing is not faith, neither is feeling faith; but believing when we neither see, hear, nor feel is faith; and everywhere the Bible tells us our salvation is to be by faith. Therefore we must believe before we feel, and often against our feelings, if we would honor God by our faith."[2]   Basic faith causes conviction and instigates belief in God.

Faith, according to Hebrews, is the confidence we have in knowing that we already possess that which we hope for, based upon the faithfulness of God and his Word. God has always been faithful to his Word, his promises, his covenant to his people in the Old Testament, and with the church in the New Testament. This kind of faithfulness calls for our loyalty, our devotion, and our truthfulness to the principles of Scripture. We are called to be true to his Word and his righteousness. All this can only be accomplished in the strength of the Holy Spirit. Our faithfulness is predicated upon the faithfulness of God.

I am sure you can bring to mind many examples of exemplary faithfulness displayed by those who have outwardly lived solely for the glory of God and the blessing of others. In the town where I grew up, we had a Christian couple who ran a small mission while at the same time tending their farm. The farm was tiny, but it was their only form of income. Yet putting their livelihood as secondary, they spent much time and energy at the mission. Inside and outside, the place was unattractive and very basic. Furniture was sparse, and often the place was cold, but that was no deterrent for this couple to always be available to children and young people, as well as those who were disenfranchised and unwanted by society, those who needed practical assistance and encouragement. The couple's sole aim was to point people to Jesus. They held regular meetings, both midweek and on Sundays. For them, numbers were of no concern. There could be three people turn up for a prayer meeting, maybe thirty children in a mid-week meeting, and perhaps fifteen people show up on Sunday. The doors were always open, and they were always available, ready to help with a message of hope and comfort. All this occurred many years ago; however, I have since learned of people who rarely if ever went to church but who have never forgotten the love and affection offered to them by Mr. and Mrs. Potts. Their faithfulness was extraordinary.

This is similar to the faithfulness we see in older believers. For them not to attend church would never be in question. There has to be sickness or some unavoidable event to keep them from their regular attendance. Some would equate such loyalty with legalism or blind adherence as opposed to an expression of faithfulness to the fellowship. Could it not be their sense of responsibility in bringing encouragement to the leaders or even their faithfulness to the Word of God in its exhortation to meet and worship?

We have all heard the statement, "I can be as effective as any Christian without going to church!" I would seriously question that. I remember the illustration of taking a piece of coal off the fire and placing it on the hearth. The coal would slowly lose its heat and become colder and colder until there was no warmth at all. It was used to illustrate what happens to Christians who stop fellowshipping with other believers. It would be most unusual for such a person to grow in grace and in the knowledge of Christian things as well as in his or her relationship with God. One does not become a Christian or even stay a Christian simply by attending church, but it plays an important part regarding our effectiveness as Christians.

There are three areas to which our faithfulness should respond: faithfulness to God, to his people, and to the Christian faith. Our faithfulness to God is in response to his faithfulness to us. The Scriptures indicate that God is faithful and steadfast. We read, "Know therefore that the Lord your God is God; he is the faithful God, keeping his covenant of love to a thousand generations of those who love him and keep his commands" (Deuteronomy 7:9). God's faithfulness is the theme of Psalm 89 and declares his faithfulness in several capacities. Paul also refers to the faithfulness of God in the New Testament, when he says, "May God himself, the God of peace, sanctify you through and through… The one who calls you is faithful and he will do it" (1 Thessalonians 5:23-24). In another place he writes similarly, "God is faithful; he will not let you be tempted beyond what you can bear" (1 Corinthians 10:13). God's faithfulness is infinite, incomparable, unfailing, and everlasting.

The faithfulness of Jesus is also a supreme example. Jesus made it plain that he came to do the will of his Father. We read, "Fix your thoughts on Jesus, the apostle and high priest whom we confess. He was faithful to the one who appointed him" (Hebrews 3:1-2). Four times in John's Gospel, Jesus emphasized his calling and purpose was to carry out the will of his Father. In spite of the anguish of Gethsemane, the suffering of the cross, and the separation from the Father, Jesus was faithful to that calling.

We must respond to the faithfulness of God the Father and God the Son by giving back through an expression of devotion and worship. We are called to be faithful to who God is, to his character and his nature. We are called to be faithful to his Word and to the ministry of the Holy Spirit. Our position in Christ brings with it a responsibility to be a faithful servant. In small and large tasks set before us in God's kingdom, we aspire to hearing the words, "Well done, good and faithful servant" (Matthew 25:23). Every aspect of our lives should reflect our faithfulness to God.

Being faithful to God's people seems to offer more practicality than faithfulness to God. Other aspects of the fruit of the Spirit are also involved as we are faithful to one another. As we offer our love, support, and loyalty, we find that patience and kindness help the implementation of that faithfulness. It also evidences our reliability, our trustworthiness, as well as our sense of responsibility to the "household of faith!" An interesting question to ponder is, "If everyone was as faithful as me, what would the church look like?"

We tend to be faithful to that which is important to us, whether it is our marriage, our family, our career, or maybe our hobby. We devote time, energy, and sacrifice in the process of being faithful. The same principle should apply to our Christian faith. Its importance should compel within us a dedication and faithfulness to our Christian walk beyond comparison. As we are faithful to God and his Word, so the Spirit of God teaches us and applies that Word to our lives. In turn, those spiritual principles become ingrained and create a change in our thinking, so that faithfulness to those principles becomes a natural outcome. No longer should questionable or compromising situations cause us indecision. The Spirit of God within us immediately sets the alarm bells ringing, and we retreat, or stand strong in opposition, as the situation requires. We live in a world that is opposed to the Christian faith, its principles and ideals; therefore, it is only by the Spirit of God that we achieve any aspect of faithfulness.

The Bible outlines the various implementation and roles of faithfulness expected in the life of the believer. It covers everything from ministry, to personal spiritual life, to relationship commitments and our devotion to the Lord Jesus Christ. Paul refers to our faithfulness in service and ministry as well as our faithfulness in stewardship and witnessing. He emphasizes our need to be faithful in prayer, faithful to the truth, and faithful in marriage. In Revelation we see believers recognized as being faithful followers of Christ and the call to ultimate faithfulness in these words, "Be faithful, even to the point of death, and I will give you the crown of life" (Revelation 2:10).

THE FRUIT OF GENTLENESS

God is gentle in dealing with his children. Christ portrayed gentleness in his character and nature. The Holy Spirit is gentle in his work upon the hearts and within the lives of all people. We too are called to gentleness.

The translation of the original Greek word for gentleness appears to be interchangeable with two other words, meekness and humbleness. The word carries the meaning of being mild, gracious, kind, and composed. It conveys a quietness mixed with patience. It can even mean modest. A sense of the word is gained as we think in terms of a gentle breeze or a gentle voice. Yet the word holds no element of weakness. It means just the opposite: "strength under control." It has been suggested that the "strength of steel" exists behind the word gentleness, illustrated by the strength of a "shire" horse used for pulling heavy carts. That kind of horse has enormous strength yet is under perfect control in performing its duties. It has also been compared to the taming of a wild horse that now responds to a bit and bridle. There is no way that the word describes spinelessness or passivity. Moses was referred to as the "meekest" man upon the earth, but strength in leadership and even anger was not foreign to him. Jesus was meek, but he was not weak.

Like me, you surely have known people who demonstrate this aspect of the fruit of the Spirit. I have a pastor friend whose first wife (who died in her twenties) was the epitome of having a gentle spirit. Wherever she went, people would recognize and comment on the gentleness of her character. It was conveyed through her speech, her attitude, and her behavior. Her very nature displayed itself in her sensitivity to people. It seemed that she always left behind a fragrance of the Spirit of God. Truly she expressed the gentleness of Christ through her life. This is the life to which we are called.

Gentleness, or meekness, is best seen in our character. Christian conversion brings about the complete transformation of our character. The integrity of Christian character should be beyond question. False character is good in appearance only. Christian character is living out the ingrained spiritual habits as they affect our everyday behavior, but the development of that character does not occur overnight—it requires the practice of constant determination and fortitude. Someone likened it to the practicing of a foreign language.

Character makes the person. When we hear the statement, "He is a nasty character!" we understand it indicates a person who is mean and disagreeable. When we hear "What a pleasant character he is!" we immediately imagine someone who has a gentle and agreeable nature. Employers look for a character reference that they hope shows the job candidate to be honest, conscientious, and trustworthy. A character is soon besmirched by any hint of lying or deviousness, and the person quickly loses credibility.

Character is portrayed in attitude. A humble or meek attitude is one where we do not insist upon our rights—a common demand today. We do not hit back when it would be natural to do so. We accept criticism, even if unjust, with the knowledge that the truth is known to God and he will take care of issues at hand. We look for opportunities to serve and are never too proud to stoop down and pick people up from the gutter. As we adopt the attitude of Christ, who ministered to the downtrodden and marginalized of society, so we must be willing to do the same.

The fruit of the Spirit forms the basis for Christian character. Behavior that displays patience, kindness, and a spirit of gentleness usually indicates that the Spirit of God is being given the freedom to live through the believer. Living in an ego-centric society, aggression and emotional self-preservation tends to be the order of the day. Gentleness is foreign in such an environment. This is why the Christian is different and needs to be different. For us, gentleness needs to be the order of the day!

A gentle spirit of meekness and humility is nurtured by recognizing our true position before God. As we recognize the majesty and supremacy of God and who we are in comparison, it instills within us a real sense of humbleness before him. It eradicates pride and causes our attitude towards others to be humble and self-effacing. God is the potter, and we are the vessels of clay being shaped for his purpose. As we are enabled by the Holy Spirit to demonstrate the characteristics of Christ in humility and gentleness, we will inevitably fulfill that purpose and become vessels made for his glory.

THE FRUIT OF SELF-CONTROL

Self-control is essential to an effective Christian life and walk. Without it, other aspects of the fruit of the Spirit cannot be displayed. A lack of self-control destroys and eliminates any good which might be achieved by the implementation of love, patience, and kindness. In fact, love, patience, and kindness create a foundation for self-control. Self-control cannot be faked, it cannot be imitated—it either exists or it does not. One can retain an element of self-control in a particular situation but not for long. The genuine characteristics of a person will always rise to the surface.

We are familiar with situations where there is little or no self-control. It results in arguments, harsh words, and destruction within families. It usually ends in broken relationships and damaged friendships. It leaves a trail of heartaches and irreparable emotional turmoil. Self-control is the power that enables us to control our behavior and emotions. It means having the ability to hold oneself back, being the master, being in total control of oneself. Self-control enables us to be able to keep our appetites and desires in check at all times. Self-indulgence is the opposite, resulting in a submission to lust, greed, gluttony, drugs, alcohol, and sexual sin. James talks about the difficulty of keeping the tongue under control, which, when used in gossip and criticism, can bring about untold and unnecessary hurt. James is quite adamant when he states, "If anyone considers himself religious and yet does not keep a tight rein on his tongue, he deceives himself and his religion is worthless" (James 1:26). Christian self-control means control of the body, mind, tongue, and attitude.

Our natural tendency is to please ourselves, to satisfy our wishes, to do what we want to do, and to have what we want to have. Our culture encourages us to provide excessive provision for our material comforts—mostly beyond what we really need. Our wants become our needs. We begin to put value on that which really is insignificant. This thinking is in juxtaposition to the Christian walk. If we adopt this stance, it can quickly move us away from our devotion to God and hinder our walk as Christians. It is said that the body is a good servant but a bad master. We must remain the master for our own spiritual benefit and for God's glory.

As Christians, we must be disciplined, be in charge of our lives, and attempt to keep the sinful nature in check at all times. There can be no wishy-washy action, no vacillating, and no insipid attitude. It is not a matter of just playing the game but a real control over every aspect of our lives. Yet we have to realize the paradox. Our self-control is really not achieved by our effort but by the work of God's Spirit within us. It is he who offers the primary spiritual support and power which enables us to display self-control. Paul tells us that "You, however, are controlled not by the sinful nature but by the Spirit, if the Spirit of God lives in you." To confirm this, he goes on, "And if anyone does not have the Spirit of Christ, he does not belong to Christ" (Romans 8:9). Such a definitive statement leaves little doubt in the reader's mind.

If we want to see a life which demonstrates real self-control, then we need to see Paul's instruction in Ephesians. He exhorts us by saying, "And do not grieve the Holy Spirit of God, with whom you were sealed for the day of redemption. Get rid of all bitterness, rage and anger, brawling and slander, along with every form of malice. Be kind and compassionate to one another, forgiving each other, just as in Christ God forgave you" (Ephesians 4:30-32). This is an excellent picture of a self-controlled life. A Spirit-controlled mind results in a self-controlled life. It provides the ability to keep our thoughts and temptations under control, lest they entice us away. We cannot overcome the flesh without self-control. Someone once pointed out that where self-control exists, "temptation can have little influence."

We face enemies within and without that would seek to destroy us spiritually. When Paul writes to Titus, he gives an insight into the attitude and action that Christians should take in dealing with temptations and the exercising of self-control. The epistle states, "For the grace of God that brings salvation has appeared to all men. It teaches us to say 'No' to ungodliness and worldly passions, and to live self-controlled, upright and godly lives in this present age" (Titus 2:11-12). It's the grace of God that offers us a safeguard against getting into situations of compromise. Our understanding of belonging to Christ, and living in service to him, will enable us to exercise self-control. We are given the strength and grace to overcome and to be in control. Yet people still say, "I couldn't help myself!"

It is difficult to be outwardly what we are not inwardly. It is only as we allow the Spirit of God to fill us and be in control that self-control can be operational. Although this is the work of the Spirit within us, it requires our cooperation. We are called to discipline and the exercise of submission to God. As we allow God to control our heart, mind, and will, it will naturally affect our desires, our choices, and our decisions. Self-control is often portrayed in moderation, having a balance in all things. It allows us to see the big picture and not just that which is in front of us causing frustration. Another word applicable in the exercise of self-control is *temperate*. Demonstrating the link between love and self-control, Paul gives a superb example in talking about love with the words, "It is not rude, it is not self seeking, it is not easily angered, it keeps no record of wrongs" (1 Corinthians 13:5). This is self-control at work.

A lack of self-control always has an adverse effect upon other people. Therefore our self-control benefits others. We should live with others in mind. The Scripture instructs, "If it is possible, as far as it depends on you, live at peace with everyone" (Romans 12:18). This calls for self-control. Exercising restraint in certain circumstances will be for the sake of others, especially if there is a potentiality of our being a spiritual stumbling block to someone else. A sensitivity to others, given by the Spirit of God, will save us from spiritual short-sightedness. Self-denial, self-surrender, self-sacrifice, and self-control are inextricably linked together in the Christian life.

Although self-control is the final aspect of the fruit of the Spirit, it is no less important and critical in our Christian walk and testimony. In the book of Romans, Paul outlines the conflict between the Spirit and the flesh (Romans 8). In Galatians, he continues his discussion on this conflict between the sinful nature and the Spirit of God (Galatians

5:16-17). He then offers the criteria for us to achieve mastery in this situation: to do those things which allow the Spirit of God to control our lives and thus not satisfy the sinful nature. He exhorts the believer to be led by the Spirit, to live in the Spirit, and to walk in the Spirit (Galatians 5:18, 25). The ultimate result will be personal spiritual growth and the ability to always exercise self-control.

Displaying the fruit of the Spirit is no minor task. Fortunately, we are not called to do it in our own strength. If that were the case, we would fail miserably. We are expected to allow the Spirit of God, who lives in us, to take the lead in our day–to-day living. In doing so, he will naturally show his real nature and characteristics, demonstrated through the various aspects of the fruit of the Spirit. We will experience changes in our temperament and attitude which will even surprise us. We will rejoice in the love, joy, and peace found within ourselves. We will be amazed at the patience, kindness, and goodness we want to express. Our attitude to those around will change as we display faithfulness, gentleness, and self-control. However, before we pat ourselves on the back or become conceited, we are—and always will be—reminded that we can do nothing without the Holy Spirit working in us. It is his fruit, and hopefully we are the channels to convey that fruit to the church and to the world.

×

QUESTIONS FOR GROUP STUDY:
WHAT IS PORTRAYED BY OUR ATTITUDE?
Reading: Galatians 5:13–26

1. How do we recognize God's goodness to us?

2. How do we express that goodness to others?

3. Explain the difference between faith as a gift of the Spirit and faith as a fruit of the Spirit.

4. What motivates our faithfulness to God, to the Christian faith, and to others?

5. How essential is self-control in the life of the believer? Why is that?

6. How can we give more freedom to God's Spirit to display his fruit in our lives?

11

WHAT THEN IS EXPECTED OF US?

"And whoever loses his life for my sake will find it."
MATTHEW 10:39

In February 1989, I met a young Polish refugee in his late twenties. He was very intelligent and very pleasant. He had just arrived in Canada. I received a telephone call from a pastor friend asking me to visit this young man, who was being detained by the Immigration Authorities in Toronto. Because of my past mission experience in Poland, my friend thought it would be good if I went to see him. He was to await a refugee tribunal hearing.

The officer escorted me to a holding cell, where I was introduced to the young man. He was keen to tell me that he was a Christian and had escaped out of Poland because he was threatened with persecution. He said he had managed to get to Vienna, where a contact had given him an airline ticket to Canada. He indicated he had lost his passport. I asked the Immigration Authorities what it would take to get him released. They told me that by posting a $2,000 bond, I could take him out while waiting for his hearing. I posted the bond and took him home—much to the surprise of my wife!

Word got out among the Christian community that he was in our home, and people wanted to help. One lady spent $300 on shoes and new clothes for him. Another bought a winter coat. Many others made contributions to his cause. Our newfound friend became a very well-dressed refugee. Some other friends, who lived in another town, found him a job, but for this, he needed to live with them. He was given permission to move by the Authorities and so moved in with our friends. Our Polish refugee made himself at home with them and began work.

About one month into this new phase, we received a call from our friends indicating that the young man had been making regular telephone calls to the United States. We suggested that it might be wise to investigate further, maybe by calling those numbers. What we discovered was most disturbing.

He had not come from Poland. In fact, he had come from Germany, where he had abandoned his wife and child. He had destroyed his identity papers on the plane to Canada. The telephone calls to the United States were being made to a girlfriend. Naturally, we became concerned about his willingness to stay around for a refugee hearing. I was obligated to give the Immigration Authorities the information we had discovered and even took him in to their office for his monthly check-in as was required. They did nothing about it, and two days later he disappeared.

We had all been deceived. He had blatantly lied to us. There was no persecution. He was very clever. He knew how to work the system. However, I think he was surprised at the love and kindness shown to him by local Christians, though it did not deter him from his self-centered goal to reach his girlfriend in the United States. We later learned that he had shared his belief with a friend of ours that he could act as he wished because God would ultimately forgive him. He was masquerading as a Christian. There was no evidence of a Christian character. That is not Christian faith.

It was saddening to read the results of a 2007 survey quoted in Richard Stearns Book, *The Hole in our Gospel*. It revealed that the lifestyle of professing believers is statistically no different from non-believers. It revealed that they admitted to inappropriate sexual behavior, gambling, taking illegal drugs, over consumption of alcohol, lying, and other activities that were certainly not in keeping with someone who identifies with the Christian faith. Many people consider themselves Christian because of where they live or because they have Christian parents or simply because they attend church. These aspects, however, have very little to do with the reality of a Christian faith. True Christians are called to be different. If there is no distinction between the Christian and the non-Christian, how can a real faith exist? The difference must be evident.

There are Christians who consider that the more you can identify with the world, the more readily the world will accept the gospel. I believe this is a fallacy. There is nothing wrong with developing and having non-Christian friends—in fact, many of us have fallen short in that area—but identifying with inappropriate activity for the sake of having those friends is never justified. It results in a negative aspect to the Christian testimony. If there is no difference in our lives, then the Christian faith is unreal and appears pointless, especially to those who expect to see a difference. People outside the church are known to have said, "Well I didn't expect that of you—knowing that you call yourself a Christian." What a damning statement that is, and how humiliating.

The Christian faith has to be authentic. It should be dynamic and meaningful, not insipid and purposeless. It's not something to be used as a convenience. It is not a game. We cannot play at spiritual matters.

The Christian gospel is a matter of life and death. It is that serious.

When we became Christians, we did not just accept a new set of rules for living or a new philosophy of life. That would simply be a self-imposed reform, like making New Year's resolutions. A genuine conversion experience demonstrates itself in a lifestyle which is markedly different from those who profess no faith. As we come to

Christ in repentance, seeking forgiveness for our sin and accepting by faith the sacrifice of Christ on the cross as the penalty and punishment we deserved, then the Holy Spirit, by taking up residence within us, causes us to become different. Our thinking becomes different because our outlook on life changes. We adopted a new worldview. Our purpose and vision for life becomes different. We now operate under a new philosophy. We operate under a new value system. As a child of God and being part of God's family, we have a completely new perspective on life, but it carries new responsibilities.

RESPONSIBILITY TO GOD

It was made clear to those of us who were in the Army that, as soldiers, our first allegiance was to the Queen. This was followed by our dedication to the Army and our responsibility to protect our country. When we become Christians, we accept a similar expectation. We carry a responsibility to God, to the church, and to the world. Our devotion to God comes first, followed by our support for the church, and then our responsibility to the world.

Our devotion to God comes with a price, and unless we are willing to pay the price, then anything further becomes irrelevant. The cost is total submission to the will of God. If Jesus' mission was to fulfill his Father's will, should ours be any different?

We begin to see that cost when we read these often quoted words, "Therefore, I urge you brothers, in view of God's mercy, to offer your bodies as living sacrifices, holy and pleasing to God—which is your spiritual worship" (Romans 12:1). It is paradoxical that we have been redeemed so that we might give to God that which we do not own. We have been purchased. The price was the death of Jesus. If we have been bought, to whom do we belong? If Christ bought us, paid for us with his life, then we are his. We cannot lose what we do not have. If we have surrendered all to Christ, then everything is now under his control and direction. We are called to sacrifice not time, money, or possessions but to offer ourselves. We must place ourselves on the altar of worship, on the altar of service. We normally equate sacrifice with pain, but the Christian's sacrifice should be one of praise. We give of ourselves, not to gain, but in response to what we already have received.

The following words of Jesus endorse the sacrificial call made by Paul in Romans. Jesus said, "If anyone would come after me, he must deny himself and take up his cross daily and follow me. For whoever wants to save his life will lose it, but whoever loses his life for me will save it" (Luke 9:23). These words may mean something different to each of us, but the practical application of them is not difficult to understand. This is not just the denying ourselves the pleasure of chocolate or coffee, as some do during the season of Lent. The cross for Jesus meant death. The cross is still the symbol of death. We are called to give our bodies as a living sacrifice and are called to take up our cross daily if we want to be faithful followers of Jesus. But what does that mean? If we have been "crucified with Christ" as indicated by the Scriptures, does that mean we no longer exist? Of course we still exist physically, but it means we no longer exist to self and the fulfilling of our self-centered desires. To deny ourselves means Christ comes first in all things, especially in our devotion and service. By taking up our cross daily, we show a willingness to identify with Christ's death and sacrifice.

The only way that this is achievable is by putting into practice what Paul recommends in Philippians when he says, "Your attitude should be the same as that of Christ Jesus" (Philippians 2:5). Adopting the mind of Christ is essential if we are to bear his image. We should seriously consider these words: "The long and painstaking process of being made like Christ is a lifestyle of dying to our flesh. We live to kill our sinful nature and worldly passions that had defined us in the past. So when we devote our lives, our selves completely to the Lord, we also make a decision to say 'Not I, but Christ' and 'Not my will but yours be done.'"[1]

We are called to relinquish control! In a sermon on *The Work of Grace*, Charles Spurgeon said these words: "We are cleansed by His blood. We are redeemed by His death and we live by His life, and therefore we are not ashamed to take up His cross and follow Him."[2]

The disciples were called to sacrifice their livelihoods when they became followers of Jesus. We may not be called to do that, but our mindset needs to be similar. We need to be prepared to die to self-centeredness, selfish ambitions, selfish desires, and the overwhelming preoccupation with achieving those demands. We need to replace all that with a passion to identify with Christ in his life, in his death, and in his willingness to sacrifice everything on our behalf. Thus we live out our salvation.

When we were very much younger, my wife and I attended several very large banquets at the Hilton Hotel in the west end of London, England. These were related to my occupation at the time. The banquets were quite ostentatious occasions held in the hotel's massive ballroom, seemingly dripping with chandeliers. At the tables, each place setting had at least four wine glasses and a large selection of eating utensils on either side of the plates. Such situations can be rather daunting on the first occasion. The knowledge of etiquette and protocol is useful in life. It teaches us how we should conduct ourselves and what is expected of us. The same is true in walking the Christian life. It is imperative that we know what we should be doing and how we should conduct ourselves.

As a new believer, it is natural to ask, "What is expected of me now that I am a Christian?" The common thinking is that a certain "performance" is now expected. This could not be further from the truth. There is no "performance" expected, just the expression of a new life in Christ. However, that expression will see some new habits and activity come to be, but it must never be seen as performance. The primary expectation of the believer is to live a life which is pleasing to God, a life which brings glory to God. This is not so much an expectation but rather a necessity. If we are to grow spiritually, then we have to deepen our personal relationship with God. We have to get to know him like getting to know anyone. We need to spend time with him in prayer and meditation. We need to read and ingest the Scriptures. Our relationship with God takes precedence over everything else. How good that relationship is will determine our effectiveness within the church and our testimony to the world.

How we live and express our faith has nothing to do with church demands or expectations from other Christians. This is a wrong perspective. Expectations on our life in Christ are purely based upon Scripture. We have already mentioned that it is the indwelling Holy Spirit, whom Jesus said would "guide us into all truth" (John 16:13). Never are we to compare ourselves with others, because others are human also. Following the rules and regulations issued by the church or denomination does not equate to the fulfilling of the spiritual or scriptural responsibilities of our Christian walk. We are always answerable to God first. Our foremost responsibility is to be followers of Jesus and to reflect his image.

The original title for this chapter was "How then should we live," a title used by many writers, including Francis Schaeffer as the title of one of his books. The question, however, is apt, succinct, and demands a conclusive answer to help us fulfill our quest to live a life displaying the distinctive marks of a believer. We need to know how to translate the internal understanding of the Christian faith into external reality. As we do so, we walk straight into opposition. If we expect the Christian faith to be without obstacles and opposition then, as Jonathan Edwards once said, we are like "a fool standing by the river waiting for the water to go by!"[3] Those who indicate that by coming to faith in Christ all problems will be resolved and there will be no more struggles could not make a greater misstatement. However, the opposition and obstacles should never become our focus. Our focus must be on implementing the spiritual behavioral pattern given us in the Scripture.

First and foremost, we are called to be holy—not a popular subject for sermons these days! Nevertheless, we have a responsibility to walk in holiness. God calls us to be holy. We have to make every effort to pursue holiness "for without holiness no one will see the Lord" (Hebrews 12:14). That's quite a definitive statement. We know that we enjoy positional holiness because once we are "in Christ" the Scriptures teach that God then sees us through the righteousness of Christ and thus through His holiness. We are seen as being holy in Christ. This is the result of Christ taking our sin and clothing us in his righteousness. We saw this earlier in the book. However, we do need to cooperate with the Spirit of God by being submissive and available for him to work in us. Our holiness is still instigated from God's side.

Jerry Bridges in *The Pursuit of Holiness* summarizes well the action of God on our behalf as it relates to holiness. He states, "God's provision for us consists in delivering us from the reign of sin, uniting us with Christ, and giving us the indwelling Holy Spirit to reveal sin, to create a desire for holiness, and to strengthen us in our pursuit of holiness."[4]

The concept of holiness immediately brings to mind that it is an impossible and unachievable state. It conjures up in the mind a life of constant failure as we seek to achieve that impossible standard. Fortunately, this is not the way we need to think. Holiness means to be separated unto God, to be dead to sin. Sin should no longer be our master. We need to recognize that all sin committed is sin against the holiness of God. Holiness is part of the very nature and character of God. Holiness is one of the attributes of God. Holiness indicates his purity and moral perfection. Therefore, it is a high calling when we read in Scripture that God says, "Be holy, because I am holy" (1 Peter 1:16). We note that it is God who calls us to holiness. We read, "For God did not call us to be impure, but to live a holy life" (1 Thessalonians 4:7). But we are not left to struggle alone to achieve such holiness.

It is true that we take an active role, for the Scripture urges us to "purify ourselves from everything that contaminates body and spirit, perfecting holiness out of reverence for God" (2 Corinthians 7:1). However, it is the Spirit of God who creates that desire to be holy and who gives us the grace and strength to practice holiness. Practical holiness is the enactment of the fruit of the Spirit in the life of the believer; so as the fruit of the Spirit is displayed in our lives, practical holiness becomes a reality. However, this does not make us any less prone to temptation and sin. But as Paul explains, "For we know that our old self was crucified with him so that the body of sin might be rendered powerless, that we should no longer be slaves to sin" (Romans 6:6). Although we aim for a life without sin, sinless perfection will never be attained. God sets the standard, he is sinless, he is holy, and he calls us to the same, but he also knows that, in this life, we will always fall short.

A wrong understanding of this call to practical holiness has caused many new believers to suffer a sense of guilt and discouragement. Living a life of holiness in a world totally opposed to such a notion is difficult and calls for much spiritual discipline. Opposition and obstacles are thrown in our path daily in an attempt to get us to abandon our goal of practical holiness. Paul prays that the Philippians "may be able to discern what is best and may be pure and blameless until the day of Christ" (Philippians 1:10). We need to seek the same discernment.

I once had a conversation with a gentleman whose denomination taught and required the strictest of holy living. However, the teaching became an obstacle in itself. Some people, and particularly young people, found this demand so difficult and overwhelming that they simply "gave up" and left the denomination. Regrettably, it was presented as an exercise of human effort. Failure was guaranteed. Such a call to practical holiness cannot be achieved by human ingenuity or strength of mind.

It is not our natural inclination. Our sinful nature makes it impossible. The Holy Spirit creates within us the desire to do the will of God, which is to live a holy life. It can, and will, only be achieved through the work and ministry of the Holy Spirit in our lives.

As long as we live, our striving for holiness will be a process of transformation. It would be most discouraging if we had to live with the constant repetitive thought, "I must be holy; I must be holy." It implies that the state of holiness we desire is always just out of reach and unobtainable. In Christ we are holy, but we will constantly be learning practical holiness. We will never be able to truthfully say "I am holy" when it comes to our daily living, anymore than we can say "I am humble." By thinking and saying those words, we nullify the state of humbleness. However, as we seek to rid ourselves of all that which is detrimental to our spiritual growth, so we will progress in our understanding and in living a life of practical holiness. Holiness should become the delight and desire of everyone of us as we seek to be the people God wants us to be.

RESPONSIBILITY TO THE CHURCH

When we become members of any organization, we expect to accept a certain level of responsibility that comes with that membership. The church is not like any other organization. Our responsibilities also do not compare. As Christians, we belong to the church universal. Being formal members of a church or denomination makes no difference. If we have adopted the Christian faith, then we are part of the church. We are brothers and sisters in this global family, and our relationship is established for us. Recognition between family members is always intriguing. I remember taking a ride of five or six minutes on an airport shuttle bus in London and before we arrived at our terminal had met, chatted with, and exchanged contact information with a previously unknown fellow believer. It has probably happened to you. There seems to be an affinity or an unspoken recognition. There is a spiritual witness between us that quickly identifies that relationship.

As family members, we acknowledge that we carry a responsibility for each other. Generally, a family would be considered dysfunctional if its members did not show love and care, or had no time for each other. Those within the body of Christ, for that is what the church is called, do love and care for each other. We weep with those who are weeping and rejoice with those who are rejoicing. We bear each other's burdens and heartaches. We share in the blessings of God's intervention. We identify with those who are suffering, with those who mourn, and with those who struggle with discouragement on an uphill road of life. This is all part of the privilege and responsibility we have in caring for those within the family of God.

One of the main evidences of real Christian faith is the love which emanates from the heart and life of the believer. Just as mentioned earlier, God's love is poured into the heart, and that love overflows to others. Those within the Christian church become recipients of that love. Paul says to "serve one another in love" (Galatians 5:13). When you serve someone, you defer to them, you deliberately make yourself subservient to them, not falsely but genuinely, so that the service is authentic. In loving, we identify with the person we serve. In loving we empathize, achieved by listening and responding appropriately.

It is a fact that to give is more blessed than to receive, a principle that applies so distinctly in ministering to one another. As we share love and encouragement, it seems to return similar blessings many times over. We give, and God rewards. We are expected to live spirit-filled lives. As we do so, our lives become filled with meaning and purpose. When Christ is the focus in our lives, when he is front and center, then we begin to live as God intended. We are instructed to live in the Spirit and walk in the Spirit. We are encouraged to keep in step with the Spirit, which means we are in the place where we can be aware of his mind on matters. It is the same as walking with a friend. If we walk ahead or behind, it is difficult to hear what is being said. So it is with the Spirit of God; by being in step, we will keep attuned to hear his voice. In doing so, we will become aware of the needs of others within the church and how we should minister to them.

Although the church consists of individual members, our actions affect the whole body. Union with Christ brings unity among Christians. Our relationship with Christ forms the basis of spiritual unity among our brothers and sisters. We share the same faith. We serve the same Lord. The love of Christ within creates the bond. It was Jesus who said, "My command is this: Love each other as I have loved you" (John 15:12). Peter also exhorted the early church, "Above all, love each other deeply, because love covers a multitude of sins" (1 Peter 4:8). The fellowship and unity within the church is critical to its ministry outside. Example always leads before words. It is essential that we individually be effective within the church before attempting to minister effectively outside the church. The integrity and credibility of the church is at stake.

We may all have differing gifts and abilities but, when Spirit-directed, they work together in unity for the good of the whole body. The illustration in Corinthians 12 outlines the importance of each organ of the body to the overall life and effectiveness of the physical body. The same applies within the body of Christ. Each member is equally important, and each gift is equally important. As the gifts are implemented, they complement each other to create unity in the body. Our responsibility is to exercise our gift in humility so that others will be blessed and God will be glorified.

RESPONSIBILITY TO THE WORLD

The church is judged not by its doctrine but by its ministry, by its capacity to reach out and touch lives where they hurt. A genuine ministry of the Spirit will do just that. It will reach out to those in need, and the church will be the channel of blessing it is called to be. As members of the family of God, we make up the church. We are the church. We are the body of Christ. We are the church that the world sees. Determined by who we are and what we do, we present the credibility or otherwise of the Christian church to the world. We are the face of the church.

We cannot live in isolation. We represent Jesus to the world. We have no option. We are in the world, therefore we represent Christ in the shop, at work, in school, in the business deal, at the bank. It's not just about being in church. If we are part of "the way," then we represent Christ to others. The question is: do we do him justice? Do we do justice to his life, his teaching, and his ministry? Do our lives do justice to the Christian faith? Our lives always affect our witness. We cannot live a life that is a sham and expect others to listen when we share our faith.

When we begin to consider what is expected of us, we quickly realize that we are not "born again" to sit back in a pew and vegetate. We are expected to grow and be active spiritually. We have "new life" in Christ, and it needs to be seen. We have been renewed in the Spirit, and our lives need to show the vitality of that renewal. They need to show that we are alive in the Spirit, alive in Christ. We are now expected to make a difference. R.C. Sproul puts it succinctly when he says, "If vast numbers of people are converted but remain infantile in their spiritual growth, little impact is made by them on society as a whole."[5] To remain passive means we have not caught the vision about the need in the world. Maybe we choose to ignore the Word of God and prefer to remain within our comfort zone. Did Jesus stay in his comfort zone? When you read of his agony in the Garden of Gethsemane, you know he did not.

"What is the greatest commandment?" Jesus indicated it was to love God and love your neighbor. At another point, he was asked, "Who is my neighbor?" By telling the story of the Good Samaritan, Jesus illustrated that it was those in need, regardless of race or creed. The act of loving will always result in doing. Our expression of God's love to others appears to be a recurring theme. This is right, because it is only through God's love, his care, and his compassion that the church can reach out to those who are hurting. We love because God loves. We care because God cares. We have compassion because God has compassion. We must see the world through the eyes of God. It is not about us—it's about those in need, in need of love, in need of compassion, in need of help, in need of the gospel and its transforming power in their lives.

We in the church have been made ambassadors for God, which means that we represent him in this world. Paul confirms this when he says, "And he has committed to us the message of reconciliation. We are therefore Christ's ambassadors, as though God was making his appeal through us" (2 Corinthians 5:19-20). Before his departure, Jesus commanded us, saying, "Go into the world and preach the good news" (Mark 16:15). For most of us, the life we live is the sermon we preach. Even if we are not evangelists, our lives carry a message. As Christians, we must be concerned for those who are searching for meaning and purpose but who are looking for the answers in the wrong places. It concerns us to see so many not even searching. They appear to be immune to the need for God, for forgiveness, and for salvation. However, that does not excuse us from sharing the gospel and our faith to those who will listen. After that, it is the work of God's Spirit to take it further.

We might consider that sharing the gospel is our primary task and that would be right, but it is amazing how many opportunities arise to do just that through a practical and humanitarian act of kindness. At times we have to get our hands dirty to earn the respect—and right—to share the message of hope and love. Practical love precedes the opening of many doors. As we go through those doors, we begin to express the heart of God, his heart of compassion, and his heart of love. Through the

Scriptures, we sense God's concern for the exploited, the downtrodden, the deprived, the poor, and the oppressed. We should be as concerned.

It is commonplace for us to respond to the devastation of earthquakes, tsunamis, droughts, famines, and other natural disasters, but it does not end there. There are disease epidemics, there are those suffering with HIV or AIDS, creating thousands of orphans and displaced people. In Africa alone, 25 million people have died from AIDS, and over 30 million are still infected with the disease. Thousands continue to die daily.

I remember being in Eastern Europe about to take a photograph of a woman beggar on the street. As she held her baby close to her, I looked through the lens of the camera. At that moment, the woman looked straight back at me through the lens. I had the overwhelming sense that I was imposing upon her suffering. The shutter remained closed. I felt it was exploiting whatever dignity she had left. She needed physical help—not my trophy photo of the poor in Eastern Europe. We must never become insensitive to suffering. We must allow the Spirit of God to create within us a heart of compassion and keep us sensitive to the sufferings of others and ask him to show us how we can and should respond.

In Albania, I saw poverty unlike any other country in Europe. In fact, it was difficult to believe that one was even in Europe. Children were in rags with no shoes, people had little food, while marauding gangs attacked the drivers and stole from trucks bringing humanitarian aid to the people. The hospitals and clinics had little or no medicines, and mothers used newspapers for diapers. Such was the state in Albania at that time. It has somewhat improved since then but is nowhere near the standard of other European countries. The church is doing an admirable job in attempting to eliminate the social and spiritual problems in that country.

Yet we do not have to travel overseas to find those in need. We can likely find them in our own town—the homeless, the unemployed, the single mothers, those who are forced to the food bank because of circumstances, and the sick, both physically and emotionally. These are the ones whose situations should disturb us out of our comfort zones. They often remain forgotten and unloved. It is of no use saying, "We leave all that to the church," because we are the church!

As we consider the needs globally, we could be overwhelmed with the enormity of the task. One person asked me, "Why do you bother? You can't take care of everyone and their problems." My answer was simply, "People suffer one at a time, and we attempt to meet their needs, one at a time." People are more than just statistics.

There is a well-known story told about the small starfish. A man was throwing these small starfish back into the ocean after a storm. A passerby questioned the value of what he was doing, considering the number of starfish that had been washed up on the beach. "Why are you doing this? There are thousands of them, and whatever you do, you'll never make a difference," said the passerby. Picking up another starfish and throwing it back into the sea, the man said, "It will make all the difference to that one!" Our efforts may be to one person at a time, but it does make a difference. In reaching out to the hungry, the poor, the stranger, we are reminded that Jesus said, "I tell you the truth, whatever you did for one of the least of these brothers of mine, you did for me" (Matthew 25:40). We should need little more motivation than that.

So, what is expected of us in this arena of destitution and suffering? We must respond. How we respond is an individual decision. We have friends who, just now, are thinking about giving up their jobs and selling their home in order to give of themselves to the needs of others. Our spiritual sensitivity to specific situations will give us direction regarding the area of our ministry. Being willing to act is the secret to moving forward. We may not have access to a large bank account through which we can financially support others, but we are responsible to God for that which we keep for ourselves. It takes little calculating to discover that in the West we hold a high percentage of the world's wealth. It should follow that funds for missions, both for evangelistic and humanitarian purposes, should be plentiful. Sadly, I read that the average giving from Christians is less than three percent of their income. Approximately half the world lives on less than two dollars a day. I have also learned that if we have a bank account and some change in our pockets, we are in the top eight percent of people in the world. We have the resources, but do we have the will? Our affluence is often our stumbling block.

When Paul writes to Timothy, he strongly urges those who have, to share with those who have not. He says, "Command those who are rich in this present world not to be arrogant nor to put their hope in wealth, which is so uncertain, but to put their hope in God, who richly provides us with everything for our enjoyment. Command them to do good, to be rich in good deeds, and to be generous and willing to share. In this way they will lay up treasure for themselves as a firm foundation for the coming age, so that they may take hold of the life that is truly life" (1 Timothy 6:17-19). This is a timely message for present-day Christians.

The mission of the church, and we are the church, is both spiritual and practical. We are called to share the message of God's love and salvation to a world that so desperately needs it. We are also called to a practical ministry of bringing hope and healing to those who are in physical need. Through the years, the church has often concentrated on one or the other. We need to do both. How we respond is a matter of conscience and practicality. We cannot all be missionaries and go overseas, but we can live a life that speaks of God's love. We cannot all deliver humanitarian aid to the famine-ravished areas of the world, but we can go into our local community to help at food banks or volunteer at a downtown mission to the street people. The possibilities are only limited by our vision.

What is expected of us? We are expected to be people of compassion who exercise integrity and act upon our convictions. As we are obedient to the calling upon our lives as genuine followers of Jesus, so we will experience the "complete joy" that the Lord talked about. If we are people whose hearts and lives have been transformed by the indwelling Holy Spirit, then we will have little difficulty in understanding our role in reaching those who need Christ and the message of the gospel.

So, whether we minister inside or outside the church, our primary objective is to be a source of blessing to others. We would do well to offer the following prayer attributed to St. Francis of Assisi:

> *Lord, make me an instrument of thy peace*
>
> *Where there is hatred, let me sow love.*
>
> *Where there is injury, pardon.*
>
> *Where there is doubt, faith.*
>
> *Where there is despair, hope.*
>
> *Where there is darkness, light.*
>
> *And where there is sadness, joy.*

Real Christian faith is not for the faint of heart. It is for those who are willing to take a stand for Christ in every circumstance. It is for those who are willing to sacrifice and suffer if necessary. It is for those who are willing to persevere and become overcomers. "Be faithful, even to the point of death," said Jesus, "and I will give you the crown of life" (Revelation 2:10).

Genuine Christian faith is for those who are willing to defend spiritual and scriptural principles in a hostile world. It's for those who are strong in faith, strong in resolve, and recognized as people of the Word. It is for those who openly express their devotion to the Lord Jesus Christ. It is for those who dedicate themselves to carrying a message of love, hope, and peace to a world that so desperately needs it. If Christ was willing to give his life for us, can we do anything less? Real

Christian faith is for those who are willing to pay whatever price is necessary to be a true follower of Christ. Are we willing for that? Are you willing to do that?

Only you can say.

×

QUESTIONS FOR GROUP STUDY
WHAT THEN IS EXPECTED OF US?

Reading: Romans 12:1-21

1. What is our responsibility towards other believers? Is it optional?

2. What do you think is our primary responsibility as believers?

3. What is our responsibility to the world?

4. What do you understand as true sacrifice?

5. Where do reading the Scriptures and prayer fit in with our priorities, and why?

6. What does consecration really mean, and can total consecration ever be achieved? How can we seek to be the people God wants us to be?

END NOTES

CHAPTER ONE

John MacArthur, *Right Thinking in a World Gone Wrong* (Oregon: Harvest House Publishers, 2009).

Paul David Tripp, *A Quest for More* (Greensboro: New Growth Press, 2007).

CHAPTER TWO

1. Hugh Ross, *The Creator and the Cosmos* (Colorado Springs: Navpress, 2001).

2. T.C. Hammond, In Understanding Be Men (London, England: Inter-Varsity Fellowship, 1961).

3. George Smeaton, *The Doctrine of the Holy Spirit* (first published in 1882, re-published London, England: Banner of Truth Trust, 1958).

CHAPTER THREE

1. Quoted by J.I. Packer in his book *Knowing God*.

2. R.C. Sproul, *The Character of God* (published by Regal Books, U.S.A. Previously published by Thomas Nelson in 1987 under the title *One Holy Passion).*

3. Hugh Ross, *The Creator and the Cosmos* (Colorado Springs: Navpress, 2001).

4. Quoted by Hugh Ross in *The Creator and the Cosmos.*

CHAPTER FOUR

1. J.I. Packer, *Knowing God* (Downers Grove, Illinois: Inter-Varsity Press, 1993).

2. Quoted by Josh McDowell in a sermon on the resurrection.

CHAPTER SIX

1. John Stott, *The Cross of Christ* (Downers Grove, Illinois: Inter-Varsity Press, 2006).

2. Ibid.

3. T.C.Hammond, *In Understanding Be Men* (London, England: Inter-Varsity Fellowship, 1961).

CHAPTER SEVEN

1. This story is taken from my book, *If we only knew... Remarkable True Stories of God's Intervention* (Florida: Xulon Press, 2009).

2. Malcolm Gladwell, *What the Dog Saw* (New York: Little, Brown and Company, 2009).

3. John Stott, *The Cross of Christ* (Downers Grove, Illinois: Inter-Varsity Press, 2006).

CHAPTER EIGHT

J.I. Packer, *Keep in Step with the Spirit* (Grand Rapids, Michigan: Baker Books, 2005).

Charles Spurgeon, *Discovering the Power of Christ's Miracles* (compiled and edited by Lance C. Wubbels. USA: Emerald Books, 1995).

William Barclay, *New Testament Words* (London: SCM Press, 1964).

CHAPTER NINE

1. Gordon Fee, *Paul, the Spirit and the People of God* (Massachusetts: Hendrickson Publishers, 1994).

CHAPTER TEN

1. N.T.Wright, *After you Believe* (New York: Harper Collins, 2010).

2. Quotation by Hannah Whitall Smith, published in *Great Quotes and Illustrations,* compiled by George Sweeting, copyright in 1985 by Word, Incorporated. U.S.A.

CHAPTER ELEVEN

1. Quotation from a blog article entitled "Devotion to the Lord" by Jossaine Galenzoga.

2. Charles Spurgeon, *Discovering the Power of Christ's Miracles* (compiled and edited by Lance C. Wubbels. USA: Emerald Books, 1995).

3. Archie Parrish and R.C. Sproul, *The Spirit of Revival* (Wheaton, Illinois: Crossway Books, 2000).

4. Jerry Bridges, *The Pursuit of Holiness* (The Navigators, 1978).

5. Archie Parrish and R.C. Sproul, *The Spirit of Revival* (Wheaton, Illinois: Crossway Books, 2000).

FREE STUDY NOTES

are available at

THE AUTHOR'S WEBSITE

http://www.jmurray.ca

For more information about

JOHN MURRAY

&

REAL FAITH

please visit:

http://www.jmurray.ca
cjm@fastmail.fm
@AuthorJMurray
facebook.com/AuthorJohnMurray

....

For more information about
AMBASSADOR INTERNATIONAL
please visit:

www.ambassador-international.com
@AmbassadorIntl
www.facebook.com/AmbassadorIntl